Applied Translation Studies

Applied
Translation Studies

Tong King Lee
University of Hong Kong

First published 2018 by
PALGRAVE

Palgrave in the UK is an imprint of Macmillan Publishers Limited, registered in England, company number 785998, of 4 Crinan Street, London, N1 9XW.

Palgrave® and Macmillan® are registered trademarks in the United States, the United Kingdom, Europe and other countries.

ISBN 978–1–137–60608–2 paperback

This book is printed on paper suitable for recycling and made from fully managed and sustained forest sources. Logging, pulping and manufacturing processes are expected to conform to the environmental regulations of the country of origin.

A catalogue record for this book is available from the British Library.

A catalog record for this book is available from the Library of Congress.

Contents

List of Figures and Tables

List of Abbreviations

AVT   audiovisual translation
CBI   China Book International
CIP   China Intercontinental Press
CUP   Cambridge University Press
DTS   descriptive translation studies
FTS   feminist translation studies
GILT   Globalisation, Internationalisation, Localisation, Translation
HK   Hong Kong
MC   Mainland China
PTS   postcolonial translation studies
SFL   systemic functional linguistics
SL   source language
ST   source text
T&I   translation and interpreting
TL   target language
TM   translation memory
TT   target text
TW   Taiwan
UK   United Kingdom
USA   United States

Acknowledgements

I am greatly indebted to Mike Baynham for the close mentoring and unwavering friendship he has afforded me over the past two years, for the many doors of opportunity he has personally opened for me, and for his wise counsel on my career and life in general. In respect of this book, I am thankful for Mike's meticulous reading of my manuscript, his advice on my Spanish and French examples, and for his insightful suggestions, which have helped me fine-tune and enhance the quality of this work.

The initial idea for the book finds its genesis in Ofelia García and Li Wei's *Translanguaging: Language, Bilingualism and Education*, published by Palgrave Macmillan. I must therefore give credit to both authors for producing such a fine piece of work, which not only enthused me into the realm of translanguaging, but also gave me the impetus to write a book of a similar nature for my field. Li Wei in particular has shown great support for my research endeavours all this while, for which I am humbled and honoured.

Special thanks is due to Mie Hiramoto for checking my Japanese examples with great care and for introducing me into Japanese academia; to Phrae Chittiphalangsri and Kanokwal Ratana-Ubol for their kind assistance with my Thai examples; to Adam Jaworski for helping with the Polish examples and for his collegial support within the university; and to Liu Zhen for his proofreading of the manuscript and his assistance with the research and logistics that this publication has involved.

Every effort has been made to obtain copyright permission for the material used in this book, although this may not have been possible or practicable in all cases. Capita Translation and Interpreting (UK), Design-lol (HK), and Gweilo Beer (HK) Limited have granted me permission to reproduce their copyrighted images in Figures 3.1, 5.1, and 5.2 respectively; and George Ho has kindly allowed me to reproduce his translations in Chapter 3.

I have had the benefit of receiving funding support from the University of Hong Kong in conducting research, the partial findings of which are included in this book. Part of my research on localisation and multilingual marketing communications for Chapter 3 was supported by the Louis Cha Fund for East-West Studies (Project code: 203810796); the research for translatorial action in crosscultural publishing in the same chapter was supported by the Louis Cha Fund for Chinese Studies (Project code: 203800730) and the Seed Funding for Basic Research (Project code: 201311159024). For all of this I am grateful.

CHAPTER 1

Introduction

Translation: Why even bother about it?

Imagine some acquaintance of yours enquires about your field of study in college; you reply: translation. In all probability you would be met with a bemused response: 'Translate what? You mean *that* needs to be *learnt*?' Such a response belies the assumption that translating as a skill comes about intuitively; it is an immanent quality of being a bilingual or multilingual person. Hence, unless you are an absolute monolingual – and such people are increasingly rare in today's world – you must be able to translate between two or more languages or language varieties at your disposal without having received any kind of formal training. It then follows that any attempt, let alone systematic programme, to teach and learn translation can only be superfluous.

And that is true – to a certain extent. Throughout history bilingual persons have been rendering texts from one language into another without having any inkling of what translation is in its academic sense. The notion of translating being a natural ability is perhaps most visible in the oeuvre of literary luminaries who **self-translate** between two languages, such as Samuel Beckett (English/French) and Vladimir Nabokov (Russian/English), just to name two of the most celebrated bilingual writers the

---

Self-translation

Normally when we speak of translation, we mean translating someone else's writing. When you write an original piece in one language, and then translate that piece into another language yourself, you are engaged in self-translation. Whereas the typical translator is more or less bound by the original text, the self-translator has a special licence to depart from his or her own writing, and even to modify the original piece in the light of the self-translation.

---

contemporary world has ever seen. Here translation, like creative writing, is seen as an innate quality, a manifestation of linguistic genius that cannot be acquired through sustained effort.

But before we set forth to claim, on the basis of this evidence, that the ability to translate is a corollary of bilingual proficiency, let us accept the plain fact that, unlike Beckett and Nabokov, most people who know and use two languages are not **balanced bilinguals**, that is, people who have equal mastery of both languages. For most bilinguals one of their two languages is dominant, typically the native tongue that governs judgements on grammatical well-formedness (Myers-Scotton 2006: 38, 295). Dominant bilingualism implies that transferring between any two languages is not usually an automatic, subconscious act; it needs to be deliberated through, which means it is a conscious problem-solving and decision-making process. At one level, translating is analogous to working out mathematical sums: we start with a problem – the original text, known as the **Source Text (ST)**, written in the **Source Language (SL)**; we apply a rigorous logical procedure to it – textual strategies and linguistic techniques; and we obtain a solution – the product of translation, known as the **Target Text (TT)**, inscribed in the **Target Language (TL)**.

Extending this, we could use a medical metaphor: we begin with a certain health issue, say a persistent headache (the ST); we visit a family doctor who applies a medical procedure to diagnose the issue (analysis of the ST and identification of textual difficulties); and this doctor comes up with a prescription to mitigate the pain (textual solutions to resolve identified problems in the ST). Yet another possible analogy is to legal proceedings: we start with the material facts of a case (the ST) and the arising legal issues (the linguistic or cultural problems residing in the ST); a court then applies principles of law possibly derived from similar precedent cases (principles of translation formulated and used in previous translations) to the facts to resolve the dispute at hand and come to a reasoned decision or judgment on the case (textual decisions on how to produce a translation). If these analogies work for us, then translation, as with medicine and law, must involve learnable skills that can be deployed in the execution of an interlingual task.

The first point we want to make is thus that for individuals who can shuttle between different languages with absolute ease and impeccable facility, translating is probably an inherent faculty. But experts in bilingualism, including Myers-Scotton (2006), tell us that such people are more the exception than the norm. For most bilinguals for whom the intricate workings of translation are less than intuitive, translation, as with other kinds of professional expertise, is learnable. It is learnable because there are explicable procedures to it, and acquiring these procedures at a conscious level can hopefully help us attain textual outcomes that are desirable in the circumstances.

This basic fact eludes the layperson who has only an illusory idea of what translation entails but with no hands-on experience in it whatsoever. So next time if someone were to express perplexity that you're taking a course in translation, go ahead and ask him or her to translate a stretch of text; unless this is a hopelessly straightforward text ('I love you'), chances are this person will hesitate or stammer in the process. Hesitation or stammering in translation is clear indication that it is not intuitive or natural, that there are barriers to be crossed, boundaries to be traversed, differences to be negotiated. If that is the case, one could proceed to argue that learning translation enables one to consciously reflect on the linguistic options available in tackling a piece of text, so as to be able to make informed textual decisions.

Learning translation, however, does not turn each of us into a Beckett or Nabokov. Just as not every learner of the piano can or needs to become a professional pianist, so not every student of translation can or needs to become a professional translator. But this should not at all discourage us from learning translation. We can learn about how the law works without aspiring to become a legal practitioner; through legal education, we come to understand the duties and obligations between individuals as well as between the individual and the state, and this understanding will help us make decisions in regulating our behaviour and conducting our businesses. In a similar vein, learning translation helps us appreciate the commonalities and dissimilarities between people from different linguistic and cultural backgrounds and equips us with the tools to communicate across languages and cultures so as to achieve our desired goals – be it to sell a product in an overseas market or simply to make the acquaintance of a foreign person.

Perhaps more importantly, learning translation sensitises us interculturally; it increases our awareness of and respect for the diversity of human species on this planet, and hopefully lessens the chauvinistic tendencies in those of us who have not been very much in contact with people different than ourselves – linguistically, culturally, and in countless other ways.

Accepting that we are seldom in an ideal state of perfect bilingualism or multilingualism, and that translation as a skill should therefore be acquirable though not necessarily to the level of an expert professional, the next question is this: what are we learning exactly when we confess, still not completely without a tinge of embarrassment perhaps, that we are studying translation in college? This deceptively simple question begs the further question of what the term translation refers to in an academic context. Translation is a generic label that encompasses two interrelated concepts, namely 'translating' and 'translation studies'. The former denotes the practical act and formal process of moving a text from one language into another – the commonsensical notion of translation. It is rooted in praxis. The latter term describes a field of study, an intellectual enterprise that takes into its purview the various approaches, theories, and paradigms that have come to shape its character.

ST-TT analysis

A basic method in translation studies, where an original text and its translation are juxtaposed and compared. The object of this analysis is to identify variances between the two texts, either to illustrate the structural differences between two languages or to elicit textual evidence to support claims that the ST has been altered or manipulated.

In some situations, there can be two or more TTs to one ST. For example, the Harry Potter novel series has been translated into dozens of languages, which allows for a more complex ST-TT analysis (ST → TT1, TT2, TT3...). It is also possible to have multiple translations of a ST into the same TL, either contemporaneously or in the form of **retranslations**; this applies in particular to canonical or 'classic' works. Further, a text can derive plural renditions for different types of audience, as for example adult versus children readers, either in the SL itself or into one or more TLs, or even for different media. These are all different manifestations of translation (this is translation in a very liberal sense, which we do not have to be too concerned with at this point). A case in point is Douglas Adams' *The Hitchhiker's Guide to the Galaxy*, a successful BBC radio broadcast that has been adapted into different modes (novel series, TV series, video games, audio editions, stage plays, feature film) in English and translated into scores of other languages.

The two are obviously intertwined: there can be no translation studies without the practical business of translating. For one thing, the primary object of translation studies are the translated texts and the original texts that give rise to them. The most fundamental method used in translation research is known as the ST-TT analysis, whereby a translation (or a segment of it) is compared and contrasted with its originating text (or the corresponding segment in this text) to identify, evaluate, or explain **shifts**. Shifts are specific instances where the translated and original texts differ from each other, the assumption here being that, by default, the two texts are bound by sameness in terms of their form and/or content.

Translation studies: The applied vs. the conceptual

We will be looking at shifts in greater detail in the next chapter; for now it suffices to note that the very idea of shifts implies an attention to the materiality of translation: texts. Early translation theorists paid exclusive attention to the text, be it its linguistic form or functional purpose. The aim of studying translation, according to this tradition, is to develop principles based on empirical data, and to employ these principles systematically to assess and enhance the quality of translation output. We refer to the theories and approaches that emerge from this tradition as **applied theories**, and the subfield that they constitute **applied translation studies**. Applied translation studies interests itself in the 'how' of translating; for this reason, it underpins the curricula of most college translation programmes, which take it as their mission to teach students the craft of translation.

It is quite fair to suggest that translation studies is grounded in translat*ing* – the *-ing* form is crucial here, for it foregrounds the concreteness of the textual act – and that translating provides the life source for translation studies. But that is not all there is to translation studies as a field, which exceeds translating per se. From the 1980s onwards, translation scholars, especially those trained in comparative literature, started to question the utilitarian disposition of early translation theories. They began to develop theoretical paradigms that examine texts not for the sake of informing future practice, but for the sake of unveiling cultural, sociological, and ideological issues that lurk behind the many microtextual decisions that go into making a piece of translation.

In this latter tradition, translating is still central to translation studies, and the method of ST-TT analysis is often still employed. In contrast to applied theories, however, the goal of culture-oriented translation studies is no longer to appraise existing translations or to supply guidelines to translators on how to go about doing their job, but rather to critique the power structures that govern the shape of translations. This critique is often undertaken within the theoretical framework of various strands of cultural studies, such as postcolonial studies, feminist and queer studies, and cultural anthropology. For that reason, this shift of analytical attention away from the sheer linguistic nitty-gritty of translation and toward the extra-linguistic factors surrounding its production, circulation, and reception is known as the **cultural 'turn'** in the field. As this direction of research does not ensue primarily in direct applications but in theory building and critical contemplation, we call the related approaches **conceptual theories**, and the subfield thus constitutes **conceptual translation studies.**

Broadly speaking, therefore, there are two dimensions to translation studies: the applied and the conceptual (Figure 1.1). The relation between these two facets of the same field is at times fraught with tension. While practitioners are largely either ignorant or disdainful of conceptual theories, cultural studies-oriented translation scholars have been critical of applied theories, which they deem to be focusing on

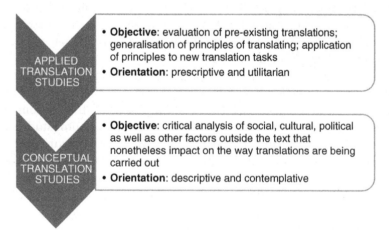

Figure 1.1 Applied translation studies vs. conceptual translation studies

evaluation and prescription ('the translator should not have done this; s/he should have done that instead') at the expense of a description and analysis of the ideological circumstances that sway or determine textual decisions.

An interesting book on the applied-conceptual dichotomy in translation studies is *Can Theory Help Translators? A Dialogue Between the Ivory Tower and the Wordface* (Chesterman & Wagner 2014). As the title suggests, the book is about whether and how theory can dovetail into practice in the translation studies field. It comprises an extended dialogue between Emma Wagner, a translation practitioner who worked for the European Commission, and Andrew Chesterman, a translation theorist and professor. The exchange between the two suggests that theorists and practitioners approach translation from different vantage points. Whereas theorists perceive their role 'as studying the translators, not instructing them' (2), practitioners expect theory to provide them with a 'toolkit of theoretical concepts that translators should bring to their job' (7). But what kind of theorists are we referring to here? The applied theorists, as we shall see, can be quite explicit when it comes to telling translators what to do; they do not shy away from prescription. As such, applied theories operate stoically at the 'wordface' rather than in the 'ivory tower' (the book's subtitle), and aim to provide some sort of 'toolkit' that translators can readily put to use. It is noteworthy that even as Wagner and Chesterman represent opposing camps, they concur on the practical usefulness of certain aspects of theory, such as classification (text type, reader type, translation purpose), translation strategies, and quality assessment – all of which are aspects of applied translation studies.

Things become quite different when it comes to conceptual theories. Conceptual theorists are not concerned with whether a piece of translation is professionally executed; nor will they devise remedial procedures to rectify perceived errors. In other words, theory and practice do not form a feedback loop. Note that no value judgement is implied here: this is by no means a sad story. Instead of suggesting that theory and practice must come together, it might make more sense to ask, apropos of translation studies, whether conceptual theories can serve a different purpose than to enhance the quality of translations. Chesterman invites us to consider the situation in other fields. He argues that in musicology and literature, theory functions to enhance an understanding of the respective arts rather than to produce more competent musicians and writers (Chesterman & Wagner 2014: 2). The question, then, is why this should not also be the case for translation studies.

Even more interesting, Chesterman suggests a thought experiment: to imagine an apparently nonsense theory, and to think about what it allows us to do. He proposes Chair Theory, an imaginary theory about chairs and a potential discipline in its own right. To Wagner the practitioner, the hypothetical Chair Theory should allow us to: (1) observe different kinds of chair diachronically and synchronically; (2) generalise, on the basis of this observation, the definitions and categories of chairs as well as the constraints of their design and production; and (3) advance principles and doctrines in relation to chair-making. The purpose of such a theory will be to provide standards and guidelines of practice to producers and users of chairs. Wagner wryly adds, as an obvious satire on conceptual translation theories, that only when Chair Theory has addressed the above can it be allowed 'to indulge in cogitation' about philosophical questions pertaining to chairs (e.g., 'Are chairs possible?') (Chesterman & Wagner 2014: 3).

Chesterman, however, has different expectations for Chair Theory. Noting that translation theory has in fact addressed Wagner's objectives, he suggests that Chair Theory can also be interested in a host of other themes that do not necessarily guide usage or production but can nonetheless still enrich our knowledge about chairs. These themes can include: 'chairs and power (thrones...), chairs and communication (seating arrangements...), carpenters' decision-making processes, the relation between chairs and other furniture, how chairs age, when they become outdated and need replacing' (Chesterman & Wagner 2014: 3).

One point that emanates from the Chesterman and Wagner dialogue is that this creature we call translation theory – which in this book is synonymous with translation studies – is a very heterogeneous entity. Hence, in their exchange, theory and practice seem to interface at some points (e.g., text-type theory) but radically diverge at others (e.g., the notion of foreignisation). This means that the question 'Can theory help translators?' can ultimately yield no final satisfactory answer, even though the process of debating through the question can be interesting in itself. After all, can we reasonably expect feminist translation theories to assist professional translators working for, say, the European Commission? Conversely, can we insist the run-of-the-mill translations churned out on a daily basis in the legal, government, and corporate sectors be of such immense interest to the theorist working on the relation between translation and postcolonialism?

The way out of this quandary is, quite simply, to recognise the applied and the conceptual as two autonomous realms within the field of translation studies. While dealing with the same subject matter, they serve very different purposes. Applied theories aim at the resolution of textual asymmetries, hence the quest for **equivalence** at various levels. Questions asked include: how do I translate this word or structure into my target language? What options do I have, and what linguistic factors should I consider in deciding on my preferred choice? Other applied theorists are interested in the actual circumstances in which translations are put into use and whether the translations achieve their **functional purpose(s)**. The pertinent questions will then be: what type of text am I dealing with? What are my clients' goals in having this document translated? Who will be reading my translation, and in what format will it be received?

Conceptual theories, too, deal with asymmetries, albeit of a very different nature. For example, postcolonial translation theorists are concerned with the unbalanced power relations between the coloniser and the colonised, or between prestigious and non-prestigious languages; feminist translation theorists resist and subvert male hegemony in their gender-based translation projects. Unlike their applied counterpart, conceptual theories do not aim to deliver optimal solutions to textual problems. Their raison d'être is contemplative, and their method descriptive, the outcome of which is a critical understanding of how translation operates under specific circumstances, without an intention to prescribe. It pursues knowledge for knowledge's sake and does not ensue in a tangible product that can be used or commodified. Therefore, applied and conceptual theories of translation constitute two distinct enterprises; each justifiably exists in its own right, aligned with what are called applied research and basic (non-application oriented) research respectively.

A qualification is in order here. Although we do recognise a demarcation between the applied and the conceptual, the relation between the two is really more nuanced than suggested above. Applied theories may be exclusively concerned with real-world applications; but it would be misguided to think that conceptual theories are divorced entirely from corporeal affairs, circulating as they do within the four walls of the ivory tower. Many conceptual theorists who are not interested in prescribing optimal translation methods are nevertheless invested in actively using translation to change the world, or rather change the ways in which people see the world. In this sense conceptual theories can have an applied edge to them (though, admittedly, there are conceptual theories of a purely meditative nature). We will return to this point again in the concluding chapter of this book.

Applied translation studies: Three paradigms

This book introduces applied translation studies, where the contemporary story of translation properly begins. Our focus throughout is on the applied, though where relevant to an applied point we may introduce particular conceptual insights to help understand and explain the practical issue at hand.

As an academic endeavour, translation started off within the context of applied linguistics. In foreign language acquisition, translation is used as a pedagogical tool, particularly in the drilling of grammatical and syntactical rules. This function is still very much with us today; in many a foreign language textbook, translation figures as part of the routine of instruction, where students are asked to translate sentences from their native language into the new language they are learning so as to familiarise themselves with its structural patterns.

Outside of language teaching and learning, translation theories have been conceived with a view to enhancing the practitioner's craft using various principles, strategies, and procedures. One focus of the theorist here is on the kinds of technical problem that might ensue as a text moves from one language into another as well as how to resolve such problems at various levels of language. Yet another focus is on whether the end-product of translation fulfils the broader communicative goal it sets out to achieve. Ultimately applied theories are grounded in translational praxis, that is, the corporeal *doing* of translation (translating) as opposed to contemplative *thinking*. This 'doing' involves the evaluation of existing translations, diagnosis of the issues involved, and prescription of linguistic solutions for the improvement of translation quality. Evaluation, diagnosis, and prescription are the key attributes of applied theories.

In the following chapters, we discuss three major paradigms in applied translation studies and their constituent theories: the **equivalence**

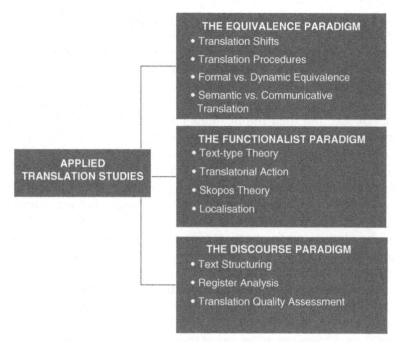

Figure 1.2 Three paradigms in applied translation studies

paradigm, the **functionalist paradigm**, and the **discourse paradigm** (Figure 1.2). In addition to explaining the important concepts and models proposed under each of these paradigms, we illustrate how they can be put to work using concrete examples from contemporary society. While the three paradigms have different foci and operate within different theoretical frameworks, they are bound by one common trait, and that is they are all eminently concerned with the 'how' in producing the preferred translation, however the latter is defined.

The equivalence paradigm is concerned with constructing equilibrium between two language texts at the level of discrete units of language, normally within the confines of the sentence. How should we translate an idiom or metaphor from one language into another, for instance? And is there only one way of doing this? We will learn about shifts and procedures from the perspective of contrastive linguistics, as well as more dynamic and communicative methods of translating.

The functionalist paradigm, by contrast, is not entirely interested in what happens inside the text; it turns its attention instead to how to make a text function to its best capacity in its circumstances. This naturally involves looking at a piece of translation not only with reference to its original text, but also in relation to the commissioners and consumers of the translation job. Themes we will be covering include: different categories of text and their implications for translating; translation as an interactional and communicative event designed for a specific purpose; and the contemporary phenomenon of localisation.

The discourse paradigm, like the equivalence paradigm, is primarily linguistic, but its horizon extends beyond the sentence to aspects of the text as a whole, including how information is organised and connected, how the attitudinal stance of the writer or speaker reveals itself through discursive choices, and so forth. Here we look at the structure and register of texts and how these are taken into account in translating and the assessment of translation quality.

In our story of applied translation studies, the paradigms and models appear more or less in accordance with the point in time when they came into being; however, there is no strict chronology as such, and the reader should be aware at the outset that there is no neat, linear progression from the equivalence, through the functionalist, to the discourse paradigms. There is a great deal of overlap, and it is merely for convenience that we present the theories as if they came about in succession. With this in mind let us begin our journey.

Further reading and reflection

1. Before we move forward, let us first move backward into biblical history and read the story of the Tower of Babel, from the *Book of Genesis*. The extract below is taken from the New King James Version (www.biblegateway.com/ passage/?search=Genesis+11&version=NKJV).
   a. What do you think is the relevance of this story to translation, even though the term 'translation' does not appear in the passage at all? We will address this briefly in the next chapter but try to develop your own argument first.
   b. Imagine we had a choice to return to a pre-Babelian era, where 'the whole earth had one language and one speech'. Does this sound like an ideal realm to you? Why or why not?

The Tower of Babel (Genesis 11)

Now the whole earth had one language and one speech. And it came to pass, as they journeyed from the east, that they found a plain in the land of Shinar, and they dwelt there. Then they said to one another, 'Come, let us make bricks and bake them thoroughly.' They had brick for stone, and they had asphalt for mortar. And they said, 'Come, let us build ourselves a city, and a tower whose top is in the heavens; let us make a name for ourselves, lest we be scattered abroad over the face of the whole earth.'

But the LORD came down to see the city and the tower which the sons of men had built. And the LORD said, 'Indeed the people are one and they all have one language, and this is what they begin to do; now nothing that they propose to do will be withheld from them. Come, let Us go down and there confuse their language, that they may not understand one another's speech.' So the LORD scattered them abroad from there over the face of all the earth, and they ceased building the city. Therefore its name is called Babel, because there the LORD confused the language of all the earth; and from there the LORD scattered them abroad over the face of all the earth.

2. Read the first chapter of the book *Can Theory Help Translators? A Dialogue Between the Ivory Tower and the Wordface* (Chesterman & Wagner 2014). A Google Books version is available here: https://books.google.com.hk/ books?id=C8wJBAAAQBAJ&printsec=frontcover&hl=zh-TW#v=onepage& q&f=false
   Even before you have learnt anything about translation studies, assess your own professional persuasion:
   a. Are you more inclined to become a practitioner working at the front line of the translation industry? Or are you more inclined to become a conceptual theorist working in the ivory tower?
   b. Whichever side you choose, reflect on what it is that attracts you to become either a practitioner or a theorist. This is purely subjective – there is no 'correct' answer.
   c. Do you think it is possible or realistic for one to straddle both sides with ease?

CHAPTER 2 The Equivalence Paradigm

Topic Map

SHIFTS	• Key author: J. C. Catford (1917–2009) • Representative work: *A Linguistic Theory of Translation* • Theory/model: Typology of linguistic shifts – (1) Level shifts; (2) Category shifts (structure; class; unit; intra-system)

PROCEDURES	• Key authors: Jean-Paul Vinay (1910–1999) and Jean Darbelnet (1904–1990) • Representative work: *Comparative Stylistics of French and English* • Theory/model: Typology of translation procedures – (1) Direct translation (borrowing; calque; literal translation); (2) Oblique translation (transposition; modulation; equivalence; adaptation)

FORMAL VS. DYNAMIC EQUIVALENCE	• Key author: Eugene Nida (1914–2011) • Representative works: *Toward a Science of Translating; The Theory and Practice of Translation* (with Charles Taber) • Theory/model: Dynamic equivalence is achieved when TL readers respond to TT in a way comparable to how SL readers respond to ST. Cf. formal equivalence, where TT remains generally faithful to the form and structure of ST.

SEMANTIC VS. COMMUNICATIVE TRANSLATION	• Key author: Peter Newmark (1916–2011) • Representative work: *A Textbook of Translation* • Theory/model: Communicative translation conveys the message and force of ST in a natural and resourceful way. Cf. semantic translation, which focuses on the meaning of words and traces the thought processes of ST author.

In pursuit of equivalence

Every academic discipline has a central problem. For economics, it is the scarcity of resources, which motivates us to find different models to allocate them efficiently. The central problem for translation studies is the inherent difference between languages and cultures. As translators, we attempt at different ways to overcome such differences; in other words, we are constantly pursuing some form of equivalence between languages and cultures. As we will learn throughout this book, there exist different types of equivalence between a translation and its original text. Equivalence requires sameness, and this means the mitigation if not the outright elimination of difference. But it is a plain fact that languages and cultures are anything but the same, especially those belonging to different language genealogies and distant geographical locations. Hence, like economics, applied translation studies sets out to resolve a perceived lack – the lack of identity between languages and cultures.

But why, in the first place, should equivalence be so desirable? The simple answer is that it allows people from different languages and cultures to communicate with one another effectively, and such communication is necessary in order for people speaking different tongues to collaborate for some common purpose. This means that in the hypothetical situation where everyone spoke one and the same language, translation as such would cease to exist. This is perhaps best illustrated by the story of the Tower of Babel which we read in Chapter 1: back in antiquity, the people of earth spoke the same tongue, by virtue of which they came to develop a strong communal identity. One day, they decided they should build a city and a tower to make a name for themselves so that they would not be scattered all over the face of earth. The prospective tower would be one whose top could reach the heaven. The project was the sign of Man's flamboyant ambition, and this angered God: if the people are enjoined by one language, they are practically unrestrained in achieving their desires. So apparently linguistic unity was perceived as a powerful resource that could lead to the accruement of excessive power. God therefore punished the people for their complacency by confounding their tongues so that they cannot understand one another.

Translation begins where our Babel story ends, even though that is not explicitly stated in the Bible: the dispersal of tongues and peoples gave rise to an asymmetry in communication that translation was destined to remedy. Throughout history, empires have been relying on translators and interpreters to negotiate diplomatic relations with their neighbouring sovereignties. And in today's globalised and technologised economy, translation is absolutely essential in bridging linguistic gaps between individuals, between institutions, and between individuals and institutions.

> ### Equivalence and shifts
>
> As the central problem in applied translation studies, EQUIVALENCE is a complex and multilayered notion. The fundamental idea is this: because languages are manifestly different from each other at various levels, there is asymmetry or want of equivalence. From a practical standpoint, this is an undesirable situation because it leads to rupture in communication. Translators respond to this by taking certain textual measures, called SHIFTS, to reverse the structural asymmetry between languages so as to construct a relation of equilibrium between any two sets of text.

Some may argue that we can always fall back on English, the global lingua franca. But that is not always the case; it would be fallacious to think of the English language as a panacea in intercultural communication. If an Indian technology service provider is negotiating a deal with a South Korean electronics company, English is hardly the solution. The Indian executives may be able to work well in English as they have a long-held tradition of learning and using English, a legacy of their colonial past. But the same cannot be said of their South Korean counterparts, whose primary language is of course Korean. One could imagine that negotiations between the two parties would need to be mediated through an interpreter, and that any agreement signed between them would need to come in two languages. The object of this bilingual arrangement is to generate equivalent versions of the same contractual agreement, on the basis of which both sides fully understand the terms of their cooperation in exactly the same way.

If we accept that translation is an indispensable condition in communicating across languages and cultures, and that the ultimate aim of translation is equivalence, the next question is: how do we actually achieve that? The answer: by effecting **shifts** between languages.

Shifting between languages

We start with the idea of translation shifts, first proposed by J. C. Catford in his 1965 book, *A Linguistic Theory of Translation*. Shifts happen when a translation moves away from its original text at some level of the language – in other words, when the TL shapes the same message or information using a different form than the SL. Catford gives us a more technical definition: shifts are 'departures from formal correspondence in the process of going from the SL to the TL' (Catford 1965: 73). Now we need to settle the term **formal correspondence**. This refers to the situation where a linguistic category (semantic, grammatical, syntactical, pragmatic, and so forth) in the SL finds a counterpart in the TL. For example, we know that pronouns are a major category found in many languages, and may come with a masculine/feminine distinction. Hence the English subject pronoun *he* finds a formal correspondent in *kare* in Japanese, *il* in French, *él* in Spanish, *er* in German, *lui* in Italian, and *ta* (written with a 'person' radical) in Chinese; and the English *she* formally corresponds to *kanojo, elle, ella, sie, lei,* and *ta* (written with a 'female' radical) respectively in those same languages. In specific instances of translation, these pronouns are often mutually exchangeable within the same series, in which case the formal correspondents are also what Catford calls **textual equivalents**: 'any TL text or portion of text which is observed ... to be the equivalent of a given SL text or portion of text' (27).

Therefore, while a formal correspondent is an abstract category across languages, a textual equivalent is a concrete manifestation of that category in translation. Formal correspondence and textual equivalence do not always overlap neatly. For one thing, an entity or category in the SL may not always find a counterpart in the TL. For example, when we juxtapose two languages in respect of our sensorial experience, **lexical** or **semantic gaps** can appear. Baker (2011: 17) illustrates this with the example of temperature. Unlike English, modern Arabic does not differentiate between 'cold' and 'cool'. Instead, the word-concept *baarid* encompasses both of these sensations. On the other hand, whereas in English 'hot' can be used to describe both the weather and objects, modern Arabic demands a distinction to be made, using *saakhin* for the heat of objects and *haar* for the heat of the weather. The implications for translating are obvious: what if one needed to say something to the extent of 'cool but not cold' in modern Arabic?

In cases of zero formal correspondence like this, certain techniques will need to be applied to circumvent the gap so as to artificially establish a relation of equilibrium between two languages; the result is that the

---

Lexical gap

A lexical gap arises where a lexical unit (word, phrase, or expression) in one language does not have a naturally occurring equivalent in another language. Lexical gaps are an issue for equivalence and can be filled in many different ways such as borrowing or calquing (see Table 2.2).

textual equivalent (the actual translation) would have to detract from the formal correspondent (in this case non-existent). We then say a translation shift has taken place.

To take another case: I have always wondered as a child what 'turquoise' (my favourite colour) is called in Chinese; it was not part of my linguistic repertoire at the time. It was much later that I realised 'turquoise' is referenced either via other colours or via figurative means in Chinese. The authoritative *Oxford Chinese Dictionary* uses *qinglü se*, literally 'blue-green colour', as the corresponding word for turquoise. Prima facie we can already observe a shift: a word has been rendered as a phrase (the technical term for this is 'unit shift'; see Table 2.1). But the more important point is this: why does Chinese have to lexicalise 'turquoise' as an in-between colour?

The most probable reason is that turquoise is not an autonomous colour category, which explains why it does not have a word *of its own*. This is not to say that as a natural colour, turquoise is unrecognisable to the Chinese, just as it would be erroneous to say that Arabic speakers cannot physiologically differentiate 'cool' from 'cold'. Our languages are selective in the way they organise our experiential and sensational realities into ordered 'boxes', and each language has its own idiosyncrasies in this regard. So whereas 'blue' and 'green' each has its own box in Chinese and many other languages, turquoise is not bequeathed its box in Chinese, thereby creating a lexical gap. The conjoining of two colour words (blue and green) into one suggests an effort to remedy this gap.

Evidence for this can be found in other indirect ways of denoting turquoise in Chinese. One common translation is *songshi lü* (other variants include *song lü* and *song se*), which compounds the word for the mineral stone *songshi* (whose natural colour is what we would call turquoise in French/English) with the word for green (*lü*). If we unpack the semantics of this word, it would amount to something like: '[a hue of] green [that resembles the colour of] the *songshi* stone.' Again one should be able to appreciate the linguistic effort involved here in trying to invoke the visual sensation of turquoise (via another colour and with reference to a mineral stone, both of which can be considered shifts) and to insinuate it into the Chinese language repertoire. This translation, however, has presently not made it into the dictionary, though it is in currency.

The fact that turquoise is described by recourse to other colours and/or entities leads us to the hypothesis that it is not a distinct cognitive category in Chinese. This example serves to illustrate that what we often take for granted as dictionary equivalents are not necessarily readily available correspondents that always already exist in a language. Where a potential lexical gap exists, a process of negotiation needs to be undertaken to align two languages in respect of the problematic word in question. Such negotiation entails shifts.

What we have done here is to tease out the shifts underlying the lexicalisation of a colour concept to illustrate that translation is not just a simple matching game, where we pick out an existing TL word and conveniently substitute it for a SL word. In the case of turquoise, the *Oxford Chinese Dictionary* has done the matching work for us by declaring 'bluegreen colour' as the equivalent, though the existence of other possible equivalents suggests that the Chinese translation of this word is still in flux. And where the dictionary does not do this for us, the onus is on the translator to implement the necessary shifts, for instance, by creating a neologism or by way of a word gloss plus an explanatory footnote.

Even in cases where a formal correspondent is readily available, shifts are still necessary to produce a grammatical or natural translation. Consider a description of white wine that reads: 'It has a citrus *nose* with *touches* of white flowers.' 'Nose' is a specialist term in wine-tasting lingo meaning 'smell'; it is a **metonymy**, as it is associated with and stands for the word 'smell'. 'Touches' is a figurative way of saying 'hints of aroma' – the technical term for this figure of speech is **synaesthesia**, that is, describing one sense in terms of another. Problems arise when we attempt to translate this sentence into a language that does not use the same figures of speech in describing the sensorial qualities of wine. Conceivably 'nose' and 'touches' can each find its formal correspondent in many languages, including those genealogically distant from English (i.e., languages that belong to a different language family); but using those formal correspondents to translate our wine sentence may lead to ludicrous outcomes.

In such situations and many others, one has no choice but to shift. Shifts are therefore a kind of remedial action that enables translators to negotiate the uneven topologies between language territories. Between any ST-TT pair various types of shift can arise, and it would do well for us to have a set of vocabulary to talk about them. For this purpose let us turn to a taxonomy of shifts advanced by Catford (1965: 73–82), which we encapsulate in Table 2.1.

Table 2.1 Types of translation shift

Type of shift		Description	Textual example
Level shift		A shift between lexis and grammar, e.g., when translating between inflectional and non-inflectional languages, certain grammatical forms may be rendered lexically. Hence, when translating an English verb phrase in the past perfect tense ('When the police arrived, the attacker *had escaped.*') into a language without this tense/aspect category, the grammaticality of the phrase would simply inhere in the TL lexis	'This text is intended for…' → *Le présent manuel s'adresse à…* (The article 'this', required as part of English grammar for deictic reference, is rendered as *Le present* in French, where *Le* is an article and *présent* a lexical adjective.)
Category shift	*Structure shift*	A change in elements and/or sequence in syntactic form	'The man is in the boat.' → *Tha an duine anns a' bhata.* (The original Subject-Predicate-Adverbial structure changes to a Predicate [*Tha*]-Subject [*an duine*]-Adverbial [*anns a' bhata*] structure in Gaelic.)
	Class shift	A change in the part of speech (noun, verb, adjective, adverb, etc.) that a given word belongs to, e.g., where a SL noun is translated into a TL verb	'a medical student' → *un étudiant en médecine* (The adjective 'medical' becomes the adverbial *en médecine* in French.)
	Unit shift	A change in the rank (sentence, clause, phrase, word, etc.) of a lexical form, e.g., where a SL word is translated into a TL phrase, or a SL phrase is translated into a TL clause	'The woman came out of the house.' → *Ženščina vyšla iz domu.* (Here if 'The woman' becomes 'A woman', the change in article would trigger a change in the sequence of elements at the clausal level in the Russian: *Iz domu vyšla ženščina.*)
	Intra-system shift	An 'internal' shift where the SL and TL have formal correspondence with regard a certain system (e.g., number, articles), but a non-corresponding item in the TL system is chosen	'advice' (singular)/ 'trousers' (plural) → *des conseils* (plural)/*le pantalon* (singular) (The singular English noun becomes a plural French noun, and vice versa, though English and French have a formally corresponding singular/plural distinction.)

Note: The examples in the right-hand column are by Catford; the descriptions in the middle column are based on Catford but further extended by me.

To identify shifts is to undertake a discursive exercise on the basis of existing texts. To prove really useful to translating, however, these shift patterns would need to be ratified into usable techniques. In their book *Comparative Stylistics of French and English: A Methodology for Translation* (first published in French in 1958, hence preceding Catford's model, but translated into English only in 1995), Jean-Paul Vinay and Jean Darbelnet give us a framework and a set of vocabulary that describe what these techniques, or **procedures**, might be. We can see these procedures as essentially different methods by which shifts are actualised in translation. Table 2.2, based on Vinay and Darbelnet (1995 [1958]: 30–42), lays out these procedures, grouped under the labels 'direct' and 'oblique' translation.

Try this

Borrowings and calques are common features in any language; they are two primary means through which a language expands its repertoire. Japanese, for example, has a sizeable inventory of *garaigo* ('language coming from outside'), comprising loanwords imported from foreign, primarily Western, languages. *Garaigo* is an open set that can expand its lexical stock as Japanese culture continues to make contact with other cultures; it is therefore a cross-cultural phenomenon.

Now, in any language of your choice:

1. Find at least five borrowings or calques. Remember that the difference between the two is that borrowings are restricted to single words while calques relate to structures or expressions. Also bear in mind the fact that some borrowed words or calqued structures have been incorporated into a language for so long that their initial identity as foreign entities may be obscured.
2. Identify the sources of the borrowings/calques you have found. Which SLs have they come from? Why do you think they have come from those particular languages? Is it because the SLs in question are richer in vocabulary, or could it be because they are economically and/or politically dominant vis-à-vis the TL?
3. Discuss why you think these words or expressions are being borrowed or calqued in the first place? Do they fill a lexical gap in the TL? (The test for this is whether there is a pre-existing word in the TL denoting the same entity.) Or are they absorbed into the TL as a result of their proliferation in social media and messaging platforms?

Table 2.2 Types of translation procedure

Strategy	Procedure	Description	Examples/Remarks
Direct translation	*Borrowing*	To borrow a foreign term to inject the flavour of the SL culture	The use of Mexican Spanish food names such as 'tequila' and 'tortillas' in a French text (When we speak of 'borrowings', we usually mean taking discrete terms from Language A and transplanting them into Language B; when borrowing across languages that use different writing systems, borrowing is often attained through **transliteration**. Cf. 'calque' below.)
	Calque	To borrow a structure or expression from the SL and translate each of its elements into the TL	'Compliments of the Season!' → *Compliments de la saison!* (Here we are dealing with a structure/expression rather than a discrete term. Note the point-to-point correspondence between the two segments here; cf. 'literal translation' below.)
	Literal translation	To directly transfer a SL text into a grammatically and idiomatically appropriate TL text, where the TL text traces the syntax of the SL text closely	'I left my spectacles on the table downstairs.' → *J'ai laissé mes lunettes sur la table en bas.* (Conceptually this is not very different from a calque, except we are dealing with a full sentence. Instances of point-to-point correspondence do not come by easily when it comes to translating at the level of the sentence, especially between languages from different language families; adjustments in word order will usually be required.)

			Examples
Oblique translation	*Transposition*	To change the word class (part of speech) of a SL lexical item, e.g., where a verb phrase translates into a noun phrase	'After he comes back...' → *Après qu'il sera revenu...* → *Après son retour...* (In the second translation, 'he comes back' is rendered by the noun phrase *son retour*, lit. 'his return'.)
	Modulation	To change the point of view in a SL utterance, e.g. from abstract to concrete; part to whole; active to passive; or positive to negative polarities, and vice versa; see Vinay and Darbelnet (1995 [1958]: 246–255) for a detailed breakdown	'It is not difficult to show...' → *Il est facile de démontrer...* (The negative construction in the SL changes into a positive construction in the TL.)
	Equivalence	To render fixed SL expressions (idioms, clichés, proverbs, etc.) using forms of expression that are *indigenous to the TL*, as opposed to creating calques	'Too many cooks spoil the broth.' → *Deux patrons font chavirer la barque.* (Lit. 'Two skippers make the boat capsize.')
	Adaptation	To turn a situation described by the SL into a *new situation in the TL*	'He kissed his daughter on the mouth.' → *Il embrassa sa fille sur la bouche.* → *Il serra tendrement sa fille dans ses bras.* (The first translation retains the image of a father mouth-kissing his daughter, which could be common in English culture but presumably less acceptable in French culture. The second translation adapts the 'kiss' to a 'hug'; hence conforming to French sensibilities.)

Note: The commentaries to Vinay and Darbelnet's examples are my own.

There is no one-on-one correspondence between Catford's shifts (Table 2.1) and Vinay and Darbelnet's procedures (Table 2.2), even though they are closely related. You may have observed, for example, that Catford's class shift and Vinay and Darbelnet's transposition describe the same kind of technique; whereas Vinay and Darbelnet's modulation, another very important procedure, does not find a counterpart in Catford's scheme. The good news is, while the two tables serve as quick reference guides, there is no need for us to get too caught up with their terminology. At the end of the day, translators seldom apply these technical terms consciously in the process of their work. A practitioner does not say (even silently): 'Okay, I think I'm gonna need to do a unit shift here, because this phrase should be rendered as a clause in my target language'; s/he *simply shifts* without necessarily even knowing what a shift is. In a professional setting, the concept of shift, as internalised by a translator through years of language education, is externalised as various interlingual procedures, executed more or less by intuition. The general notions of shift and procedure are therefore more important than the specific labels attached to them, though such labels do enable us to reflect on them in a more systematic way.

Another reason why we need not be obsessed with the particulars of jargon is that their usage is not always standardised. 'Transposition', as used by Vinay and Darbelnet to denote word-class change in translation, is now often used broadly to refer to semiotic transfer that involves some transformation in content, form, or even media (here it is no coincidence that we see a recurrence of the prefix *trans-* in 'translation', '*trans*position', and '*trans*formation'). Even more problematic is the term 'equivalence', used by Vinay and Darbelnet to describe the procedure of replacing one idiomatic expression with another; the term has since developed a very different trajectory (more on this below) and is now infrequently used in the sense of idiomatic translation.

We should also note that these procedures sometimes overlap and compound one another. Vinay and Darbelnet (1995 [1958]: 42) give us the example of a door sign inscribed with 'Private' and its French counterpart *Défense d'entrer* ('no admittance'). If we look at the French as a translation (we can do it the other way around), we could say that the adjective 'private' is turned into a noun structure; that a statement ('this is private space') is turned into an implied imperative in the negative ('do not enter'); and that it is not the language per se but its pragmatic situation – what linguists call **speech act** – that is being translated. This is transposition, modulation, and equivalence all at work in the same specimen of language; but in actual translating, one would almost never apply these procedures in a discrete manner.

On top of all this, there are many cases where we are simply unsure where they should be pigeonholed into either of the two tables. Thus, instead of dwelling and drowning in the conceptual terms, it may be more profitable for us to focus on two key parameters in respect of shifts and procedures. First, each shift/procedure is applicable to one of three planes of expression, namely lexis, syntactic structure, and message (Vinay & Darbelnet 1995 [1958]: 41). In other words, when speaking of a shift or procedure, we may be talking at the level of a single word, a phrase/clause, or an utterance in its entirety; these are sometimes called different **units of translation**. Second, a shift/procedure may be obligatory or optional. A shift is obligatory when it is required by the structure of the TL; not effecting the shift in question would result in an impossible structure. This situation is called **servitude** (15–16), and normally involves unalterable rules of grammar such as gender inflection, verb conjugation, agreement, and so forth.

Let us look at a few examples. English gerunds need to be translated into French infinitives or nouns, instead of the present participle: 'Dancing is difficult' → *Danser est difficile* or *La danse est difficile*, where *danser* and *la danse* are infinitive and noun forms respectively. So we might say we are doing a mandatory class shift or transposition here, though the jargon is ultimately immaterial. Many European languages are grammatically more precise than English, such that translating from English into these languages involves certain obligatory moves. For example, the English verb 'to be' translates into Spanish in one of two ways, depending on whether the state of being described is transient or permanent; hence: 'You <u>are</u> beautiful' is <u>*Eres*</u> *bella*, where *eres* is the second person conjugation of *ser*, the verb 'to be' denoting a permanent state; however, 'We <u>are</u> very well' is <u>*Estámos*</u> *muy bien*, where *estar* is the counterpart verb 'to be' pointing to a changeable state.

There are cases in Italian–English translation where a present tense form is the equivalent of a future tense form, as in <u>*Prendo*</u> *un caffè* → <u>*I'll*</u> *have a coffee*. This happens too in Japanese–English coupling. If you say *kasa-o-sagashimasu* ('umbrella-[object marker]-look for'), even though *sagashimasu* is a simple present tense form, you would effectively be saying: 'I'll be looking for an umbrella.' In Japanese, when a present tense form like *sagashimasu* is used in context, it indicates a course of action in the near future, or perhaps even immediately following the time of speaking. So if you're advising a shop assistant 'I'm looking for an umbrella', *sagashimasu* would not be quite appropriate despite its present tense form – unless you actually mean to say you're not buying any umbrellas now but a bit later! Instead we would use *kasa-o-sagashi-te-imasu*, where the conjugation *te-imasu* implies a present progressive aspect corresponding to 'am ... (look)ing (for)'. As these shifts are often not a matter of choice, they belong more properly to the province of foreign language acquisition.

In contrast to servitude is **option** (Vinay & Darbelnet 1995 [1958]: 15–16). This means non-mandatory shifts or procedures in producing a linguistically acceptable translation. We might characterise the difference between option and servitude with a hypothetical response of a native speaker in the TL: for option, this person would exclaim, 'Yes, that's exactly what you *would* say [to express the same meaning in the SL]' (37; emphasis added), whereas for servitude, it would be something like, 'Yes, that's exactly what you *must* say'. For example, a relative clause in English can be rendered in Chinese either as a pre-modifier or as a separate clause following the modified segment. The choice between the two syntactic options is dictated by stylistic concerns: the rule of thumb is that if the modifier phrase is considerably lengthy, a translator would do well to turn it into a separate clause (i.e., a unit shift). However, if the intention is to produce a **translationese** effect, then a translator could well opt for the pre-modifying option, precisely because it disturbs the linguistic norm of modern Chinese.

It is thus not difficult to see that the substantive difficulties in translating come from option. Obligatory shifts are structural, static, and predictable. These shifts are programmable into translation software such as Google Translate. Non-obligatory shifts, however, involve subtle factors and require decision-making and skilled intervention on the part of the human translator. For this reason alone, option is much more interesting for applied translation studies because it reveals the intricate processes involved in language transfer beyond the sheer mechanics of grammar and syntax. Machine translators could very well take care of the obligatory shifts for us (i.e., they are in 'servitude'!), but the rest is up to the human translator.

Translationese (or translatese)

A stilted linguistic style in the TT that constantly reminds the reader that s/he is reading a piece of translation, rather than a piece originally written in the TL. It is normally the result of borrowings, calques, and literal translation (see Vinay & Darbelnet's 'direct translation' in Table 2.2), and also the transfer of SL collocations into the TL. Translationese is *not* ungrammaticality; a TT inflected with translationese can well be perfectly grammatical, though it would sound unnatural to TL native speakers.

To language purists and most conventional practitioners of translation, translationese is seen as a hallmark of defective translation, a result of negative transfer and interference from the SL. It is symptomatic of the 'tyranny of the source language', as one author puts it; it constitutes a stylistic species of its own, a kind of **third language**.

How does the translator come to be trapped in this third language? Often it is because, having read – and understood – the original text he assumes both that everything said needs to be said and that nothing has been omitted in the source language that might be required in the target language. In other words, he sees the original text as being *complete*, and hesitates to add to it or reduce it in length. (Duff 1981: 116)

However, some scholar-translators working in the postcolonial and post-structuralist traditions, such as Lawrence Venuti, celebrate translationese as an expression of defiance against the hegemony of languages of prestige, notably the English language.

Charges of 'translationese' assume an investment in specific linguistic and cultural values to the exclusion of others. Hence close translation is foreignizing only because its approximation of the foreign text entails deviating from dominant receiving values. (Venuti 2008: 120–121)

In other words, translationese carries a stigma not because it is inherently distasteful, but because it is deemed to have deviated from some assumed norm, namely fluency. In the hands of agentive translators such as Venuti, translationese can be turned into a weapon of resistance (against global lingua francas) and empowerment (of languages of lesser prestige). Here we have an example of how a cultural-ideological perspective on translation can be brought to bear on translation practice.

As a final example, listed below are different words for 'walking' in English and their common Japanese equivalents:

'waddle': *choko-choko aruku*
'trudge': *teku-teku aruku*
'trot': *toko-toko-to aruku*
'lumber': *doshi-doshi aruku*
'plod': *tobo-tobo-to aruku*
'stroll': *bura-bura aruku*
'stagger': *yota-yota aruku*
'toddle': *yochi-yochi aruku*

(Tsujimura 2014: 388 with minor edits)

Here we are dealing with semantics. It is said that the nuances of the English verbs describing different manners of walking are not lexicalised in Japanese, but expressed by attaching an adverbial mimetic word (*doshi-doshi, bura-bura*, etc.) to the generic stem *aruku* ('to walk'). Even though *aruku* alone can translate the general idea of walking, to translate each of the English words above as *aruku* is to **undertranslate**, as the resultant TT would be expressing less information than the corresponding ST. To translate 'stagger' as *yota-yota aruku*, then, is to effect a unit shift, as a single word is translated into a phrase. And since the difference involved is structural and systematic, we might proceed to say the shift/procedure in question is obligatory.

But a wiser formulation might be to say it is *more or less* obligatory, and that is because not performing the shift does not yield an untenable construction. There is also nothing to suggest that the nuances of 'lumber', 'trudge', and so on cannot be expressed by other means in Japanese or in any other language for that matter, such as by way of simile or metaphor ('to walk in the manner of …'), especially in a literary context. Any one of these possible moves entails a different kind of shift, which means the English–Japanese pairs above do not strictly speaking illustrate obligatory shifts. Servitude and option should therefore be seen as two points on a cline rather than as two dichotomous terms, where some shifts are more obligatory than others. Unless we are talking at the most fundamental levels of grammar and syntax, the translator will typically have some room for linguistic deliberation, which means s/he will constantly be weighing and sliding between servitude and option.

The important lesson to be drawn from the servitude-option cline is this: translators must take into account the options available to ST authors and the motivations underlying the linguistic selections made out of those options. They must also be cognizant of the constraints on their own choices imposed by the TL and undertake procedures that lead to *justifiable* shifts – that is, shifts that express the intentions of the ST author (which motivated the SL choices in the first place) as fully as possible – while simultaneously observing obligatory moves in the TL.

Formal vs. dynamic equivalence

Shifts and procedures are primarily textual matters; they pertain to the matching of two languages, encompassing a whole range of translation units – morpheme, word, phrase, clause, sentence. At about the same time Catford published his shift model, an important figure in translation studies was championing a theory that had a completely different premise. Let us begin by considering the well-known (translated) expression 'Vanity of vanities, all is vanity' from Ecclesiastes. What if I were to tell you that the following alternatives are possible and that they all originate in the same ST?

1. Life is useless, all useless (Today's English Version)
2. Nothing makes sense! Everything is nonsense (Contemporary English Version)
3. Nothing is worthwhile, everything is futile (Living Bible)

(Nida 2003: 85)

These expressions look starkly different from 'Vanity of vanities, all is vanity', which follows the structure of the original Latin text closely. Yet they are said to be viable translations in their own right. This brings us to the theory of Eugene Nida, a foremost expert in Bible translation who formulated his principles based on his work in the American Bible Society.

Nida's major contribution lies in his proposal to move the focus of translating from equivalence in terms of **form** to equivalence in terms of **effect**. Hence the two key terms in applied translation studies, namely **formal equivalence** and **dynamic equivalence**. In his *Toward a Science of Translating*, Nida defines formal equivalence as the situation where 'one is concerned that the message in the receptor language should match as

---

On Bible translation

We have used a simple example from the Bible to commence our discussion of Nida's theory, but the translation of the Bible is immensely more complex than just from Latin. It was always a complex scholarly enterprise potentially involving more than one source language. The King James Bible, for example, translated the New Testament from Greek and the Old Testament from Hebrew and Aramaic.

It is also noteworthy that some of the greatest translation traditions stemmed from the ecclesiastical desire to disseminate scriptural texts. Just as the genesis of Western translation theory is inseparable from the Bible, so translation in China attained one of its highest points by virtue of translating Buddhist texts on the grandest scale ever.

---

closely as possible the different elements in the source language' (Nida 1964: 159). Here 'message' does not refer only to the abstract informational content in the ST, but also to the linguistic form in which it is expressed – the 'different elements' of the SL. A word-for-word gloss is an extreme instance of formal equivalence; in most cases, however, a gloss is not a feasible option, so more often than not we are aiming instead at literal translation, where minor adjustments are made to accommodate the TL structure (cf. Vinay & Darbelnet's version of literal translation in Table 2.2). Formal equivalence can thus tolerate most of Catford's shifts, given that the integrity of the SL is kept intact. As such, the examples listed in Table 2.1 can be said to illustrate formal equivalence at work.

Contrast this with dynamic equivalence, where 'one is not so concerned with matching the receptor-language message with the source-language message, but with the dynamic relationship' (Nida 1964: 159). And what is the essence of this 'dynamic relationship'? Nida explains that dynamism as such is determined by equivalence of reception or *response*: 'the relationship between receptor and message should be substantially the same as that which existed between the original receptors and the message' (159). To put this in another way, dynamic equivalence is 'the degree to which the receptors of the message in the receptor language respond to it in substantially the same manner as the receptors in the source language' (Nida & Taber 1969: 24). Here the objective is

---

The closest natural equivalent
Arguably the most important tenet in Nida's theory, finding the closest natural equivalent means, in practical terms, to translate to this effect: we first identify how a SL reader will most probably respond to a certain ST (e.g., s/he might find it entertaining, or feel emotionally disturbed, and so on); then, we carefully choose strategies and techniques to ensure that the TL reader, upon reading the TT, responds in the same way, or at least in the most similar way possible.

---

to obtain 'the closest natural equivalent' (13) in a way that accords with the conventions of TL usage.

A classic example of dynamic equivalence is Nida's proposal to translate the biblical expression meaning 'greet one another with a holy kiss' into modern-day English as 'give one another a hearty handshake all around' (Nida 1964: 160). This might come across as a controversial suggestion, especially in a biblical context, where the word of God is sacrosanct. The history of translation tells us stories of Bible translators being persecuted by the Church for allegedly misinterpreting God's message through their less-than-literal translation. On what basis, then, could we justify substituting a hearty handshake for a holy kiss?

Nida's position is that Bible translation is not about establishing a discursive relationship between reader and text (i.e., the actual words in the Bible); it is rather about establishing a personal relationship between reader and God (see Gentzler 2001: 52). This means the reader must be able to comprehend the Bible within the context of his or her own language and culture, and *respond* to any given text segment in the desired manner. A kiss, even a 'holy' one, may work in one culture as a form of greeting, but may come across as strange or even offensive in another. Recall Vinay and Darbelnet's example of adapting the English sentence 'The father kissed the daughter on the mouth' into a different gesture of greeting (holding the arms) in the French translation (see Table 2.2), presumably because kissing on the mouth is not being practised as an unmarked gesture of greeting in French culture. And just as in Maori, Inuit, and Arab cultures, people touch or rub each other's noses as a gesture of greeting, so in contemporary Euro-American cultures, we could do fist-bumping or high-fiving in informal settings. Yet in Thailand people place their closed palms near their chin, nose, or forehead (the specific position depending on the relative status of the addressee), while in Japan the tendency is to give a light bow (a deep bow if it is a social superior you are greeting).

So the act of greeting is a very culture-specific one indeed, and this has textual ramifications when we express it in language. Let us come back to the holy kiss-to-hearty handshake example. If we were to forcibly transplant 'a holy kiss' into a TL culture where this would not be recognised or accepted as a gesture of greeting, our TT readers would not be able to respond to this text fragment in the same way as would their ST counterparts. For example, TT readers might feel uncomfortable or disconcerted, even angry, with the act of kissing-as-greeting, rather than feel empathy. When that happens, the TT would have a different effect on its readers, as compared to the effect that the ST had on the original audience. Formal equivalence is achieved at the expense of dynamic equivalence, and to Nida that is most undesirable.

Try this

Extending Nida's 'hearty handshake' example, now imagine a movie with the title *I Am Not Madame Bovary*. For present purposes let us look only at the title, setting aside other considerations such as the plot or theme of the movie (these will come into play under the functionalist paradigm in Chapter 3).

1. If this movie were to be shown in a culture where Madame Bovary is not a familiar figure (and if you have not heard of or do not know the origin of this name, Google it now), what problems would you anticipate with the title?

2. What is your opinion on the following proposition: 'Madame Bovary is to French literature as Lady Chatterley is to English literature; therefore they can be constructed as dynamic equivalents'?

3. Suppose a Russian translator decides to substitute 'Anna Karenina' for 'Madame Bovary' in the Russian title of the movie (again, if you do not know who Anna Karenina is, Google her – the name, I mean). With reference to Nida's theory, discuss if you have any reservations about the Russian title.

I Am Not Madame Bovary is not in fact an imaginary title; it is the translation of a Chinese movie title, *Wo bu shi Pan Jinlian* ('I am not Pan Jinlian'), where Pan Jinlian is the belle infidèle par excellence in Chinese literature.

Dynamic equivalence therefore dictates that we do not aim to transfer meaning at the level of the word. To this end, Nida advances a three-step procedure (Nida & Taber 1969: 33 *passim*):

Step 1: **Analysis.**
First, we go beneath the *surface structure* ('greet … with a holy kiss') of a ST segment and reach for a more fundamental layer of meaning, which in this case is the pragmatic intention of a piece of text in the Bible. Note that what is captured here is an invariant, abstract concept ('a gesture of greeting'), not a palpable linguistic formulation. It can also involve reducing ST structures to base forms, called **kernels**, so as to catch at their core essence.

Step 2: **Transfer.**
Then, we move this abstract concept from the SL culture to the TL culture, and ask the question: what would be an equivalent gesture of greeting in the TL culture, one that can elicit the same response from TL readers? Our answer is still in its pre-linguistic state, a kind of potential form (the idea 'the social convention of greeting in the TL culture=handshaking', but yet to be properly verbalised).

Step 3: **Restructuring.**
In this final stage, we turn this potential form into a well-structured piece of TL, deriving 'give … a hearty handshake all around'.

There is the question of how translators can evaluate the response of the TT reader before a translation has actually been read. Most of the time, this would have to be an informed guess, as the translator is supposed to have an intuitive sense of the TL, and could arguably serve as an 'implied' or 'ideal' TT reader. However, the assessment of reader reception can also be based on more empirical grounds. A translator of Shakespeare's plays reports that he would observe the audience's immediate reaction to gauge whether his translation of the bard's wordplays is successful: 'Every time the translated work is performed for the first time, I would watch the audience's response to see how the words work on them' (Cole 2016: 19).

Dynamic equivalence at work: Some illustrations

Even though dynamic equivalence was first conceptualised on the basis of scriptural translation, it is an extremely powerful theory that can be used to formulate translational strategies and evaluate translational phenomena in the secular world. Take, for example, the fantasy novel series *Oksa Pollock*, the French answer to the Harry Potter series. When *Oksa Pollock* was translated for an Anglophone audience, one of the major challenges for the translator Sue Rose was how to translate the humour embedded in made-up names. A quick way out of this is to simply borrow the French names and plant them straight into the English translation. This is surely convenient but quite unsatisfactory, given that the French names are installed with all kinds of language-specific turns; these turns generate a humorous effect that is intuitive to French readers. Following Nida's theory, the object of translation here is to create new names that English-language readers can resonate with in the same way as French-language readers respond to the original names. This does not mean throwing the ST out of the window and inventing novel English names out of thin air – that would not be satisfactory either. The best translation is derived by analysing a SL name to its deep structure, transferring this to the TL culture, and then restructuring it into a viable name in the TL with an equally humorous effect.

There are many instances of this happening in *Oksa Pollock*. For example, the character name Foldingot/Foldingote is translated as Lunatrix/Lunatrixia. Sue Rose explains her rationale as follows:

> The French – Foldingot and Foldingote – is a combination of *foldingue* ('crazy') and *dingo* ('nutcase'). There are girl and boy Lunatrixes, which in the French is shown by the 'e' ending for the girl, so whatever I came up with had to be able to be varied for male and female. We often add 'ess' in English to names to show they are female, but that didn't work here. What I came up with was Lunatrix, which is a combination of 'loony' (since they're crazy little characters) and 'tricks' (for their weird abilities and the tricks they always have up their sleeves). They also have very large, moon-like, eyes and the first part of the name sounds like 'lunar'. It was then easy to add an 'a' on the end to make the female form.
>
> (Rose 2015: 18)

Even though Rose does not use theoretical terms here, she is effectively putting dynamic equivalence into action. By deconstructing the French names into their component parts, she derives two kernels: 'crazy' and 'nutcase'. These are then transferred to the side of the TL, where 'loony' (think of this as a pre-linguistic notion at this point) has basically the same idea. The translator also innovates by coming up with a new kernel – the idea of trickiness. But this is not a random choice, for it is based on the translator's understanding of the character traits of Foldingot/Foldingote in the original novel and also connects well with the idea of being crazy or loony. The translator then restructures these kernels in accordance with the phonetic qualities of the TL: hence, 'loony' (as an idea) becomes 'luna' (as a concrete form), and 'tricks' becomes 'trix'. This replicates the morphological structure of the ST (*foldingue+dingo*), while enabling English readers to respond to the evoked sounds in a similar way as French readers do.

Notice in particular that with 'luna', the translator adds further value to the ST, as 'luna' evokes 'lunar' (moon), pointing to a physical feature of the character that is not represented in the original French name. The translator also manages to reproduce the gender distinction in the pair of French names by using a different suffix that fulfils the same grammatical function in English names (consider Alexand<u>er</u> and Alexand<u>ra</u>). As a result of these procedures, the translated names are dynamically equivalent to the French names: they are rooted in the English phonological system and yet correspond to the ST both conceptually and structurally. The outcome is a clever rendition of the quirkiness of the French names that would entertain English readers.

Let us move on to a longer stretch of text. The February 2017 issue of the *National Geographic* uses this tagline in its English edition: The Birth of Booze. Our 9,000-Year Love Affair with Alcohol. What textual considerations come into play when we analyse this tagline with a view to translating it? First, we see an alliterative play in the main line (<u>b</u>irth of <u>b</u>ooze); and second, the tone is deliberately casual ('booze' instead of 'alcohol', and 'love affair' of course). The overall effect on the English reader is one of light-heartedness. Applying the idea of dynamic equivalence, are we able to reproduce this effect for the TT reader? Let us compare a few versions of this tagline.

The Spanish translation: *Alcohol. Un romance que ha durado 9000 años.* The second line displays high fidelity: 'a romance that has lasted 9000 years'. The first line is reduced to 'Alcohol'; the question is why. *Trago* could well substitute 'booze', and 'birth' could be rendered more literally as *origenes* ('origins'), hence: *Origenes del Trago* ('origins of booze'). The latter is indeed a common collocation, for example, *Origen del trago Margarita* – 'origin of the drink Margarita'. To retain the metaphorical sense of 'birth', we could use *Nacimiento* as in *Nacimiento de la Civilisación* ('birth of civilisation'), hence: *Nacimiento de un Trago*. This keeps both the metaphor and the colloquialism in the original, and is a possible formulation, though it seems less ubiquitous than *Origen del trago*.

So we have a situation whereby the most lexically and semantically accurate translation is not the most typical expression one would use in Spanish, and that alone might be sufficient reason to eliminate it as a contender. As for *Origenes del Trago*, although it is semantically accurate and widely used, it compromises on the alliteration in the ST. Since the rhetorical play in the original would have been lost anyway, this might have motivated the editor/translator to opt instead for the one-word 'Alcohol', which sounds neat and crisp and arguably gives rise to its own rhetorical effect. This is strictly speaking not dynamic equivalence in Nida's sense, as there is explicit deletion of a content word. But it does prompt us to speculate about possible decisions that go behind textual transformations, especially where language-specific rhetoric is involved.

Compare this with the first line in the German edition: *Prost!* ('Cheers!') Is this dynamic equivalence? Again, not strictly speaking, but if we consider the colloquial thrust of the English 'booze', then perhaps it might not be such a stretch to say that the interjection *Prost!* is dynamically equivalent to 'booze', for both words are intimately bound by the alcoholic theme. The determination of whether a translational intervention counts as dynamic equivalence or creative transposition is not an exact science. For an intervention to count as a translation, even in the most liberal sense of the word, the objective test is whether there is a core essence threading across two texts. In this case, *Prost!* passes the test.

The Japanese version is interesting in yet another way; the second part of the tagline reads: *ningen-tono nagaku-te fukai naka* ('long and deep relationship with humans'). On the face of the language, there is significant deviance from the English formulation. In Japanese there are various dictionary equivalents for the phrase 'love affair'. The *Kenkyusha's New Medium-Volume English-Japanese Dictionary* provides three options: (1) *ren-ai*; (2) *uwaki*; and (3) *jouji*. The first word refers exclusively to romantic relationships between people, and although in the English 'love affair' too is rhetorically extended to describe a relationship between the human race and alcohol, to do a similar stunt in Japanese would lead to a very bizarre formulation. A single structure may yield completely different reactions from native speakers of different languages, and this really is the entire point about dynamic equivalence. Professional translators must attune themselves into the *sensibilities* and *sensitivities* of their working languages so as to mediate them effectively.

The second and third Japanese words have a racy feel to them, connoting illicit or adulterous love. Of course we would say that in English 'love affair' does have a similar negative sense ('he has an affair with a woman'), but in this particular tagline, there is no such implication – the phrase is merely used in an irreverent way to suggest how we have been obsessed with alcohol throughout the history of mankind.

The phrase *fukai naka* as used in the Japanese edition translates literally into 'deep relationship'; this is an idiomatic expression that metaphorically suggests intimate, romantic relationships without a negative connotation. On this ground it is superior to any of the dictionary equivalents for 'love affair' listed above. The descriptive adjective *nagai* ('long') substitutes '9,000 years' in the English. Notice also that whereas the English uses the possessive pronoun 'our' in relation to 'love affair', the Japanese depersonalises this to *ningen-tono* 'with humans'. Taken together, *ningen-tono nagaku-te fukai naka* implicitly translates what is explicit in the English tagline. Its indirect and detached tone conforms to Japanese verbal etiquette.

A tactically different strategy is seen in the traditional Chinese version. Here the word 'love-affair' is deleted. To literally suggest a 'love-affair' (*lianqing*) with an inanimate object goes against the grain of Chinese linguistic convention. This deletion is compensated with the verb *yunniang*. The word means 'ferment' and is associated with winemaking; but it can be metaphorically extended to refer to an abstract entity in the making – including romantic relationships. But instead of 'love affair', the verb takes as its object *renlei wenming* ('human civilisation'), hence: 'Fermenting 9,000 years of human civilisation'. Here the Chinese translation demetaphorises 'love affair' and explicates its meaning, but inserts its own metaphor with 'fermenting'.

By contrast, the simplified Chinese edition manages to sneak the love theme into its translation with a nice metonymic twist: *beizhong tanlian jiuqian nian*, or '9,000-year obsession inside a glass', where 'glass' stands in for alcohol. The verb *tanlian* ('greed-love'), usually describing excessive desire for the vices, is surprisingly apt here in connection with the drinking theme and also with the long duration involved – there is the possible suggestion that nine millennia of alcohol drinking on the part of the human race is excessive, though in a cheeky rather than sombre sense here. Like the Japanese version, the two Chinese translations replace the original with expressions that resonate very well in the TL, while still accurately transmitting the proposition in the English line. All three versions may therefore be considered exemplars of dynamic equivalence.

Although dynamic equivalence is a microtextual intervention, we might also venture to look at it more broadly to tease out its conceptual applications. For this we look at the word-concept *kopitiam* ('coffee-shop') from Singaporean *parole*. This is a transliteration of a southern Chinese dialect word. It refers to a unique culinary establishment in Singapore, where different food stalls selling mostly local fare are concentrated in a designated space. A *kopitiam* is sheltered but not air-conditioned, and there are no waiters or waitresses: customers are normally expected to serve themselves by queuing up for the food item of their choice in front of the respective stall.

Consider how we might translate a text, written in any one of the four official languages in Singapore (Malay, Mandarin Chinese, Tamil, and English), carrying the term *kopitiam*. It is easy enough to find a formal correspondent for the word – many languages can come up with a morpheme-to-morpheme translation ('coffee' + 'shop'), and for alphabetic languages we might simply use 'coffee shop' as a sort of borrowing. But such translations would fail to work insofar as they do not refer to an establishment that is recognisable to the TT reader.

One might propose the café, a global phenomenon, as a substitute for the Singaporean *kopitiam*. This sounds like a convenient solution but falls short of a good translation because the café, à la Starbucks, equally ubiquitous in Singapore, does not convey the 'grassroots' or less glamorous character of the *kopitiam*. A local person feels differently toward the notion of *kopitiam* than to that of a Western-style café; hence, translating *kopitiam* as *café* compromises our criterion of dynamic equivalence. In order for the translation to have the same effect on TT readers as *kopitiam* would have on Singaporean readers, we need to find an equivalent establishment that has the same relative rank in the target culinary culture. To give an illustration: suppose we are translating an English article using the word *kopitiam* into Chinese for a Hong Kong readership. In Hong Kong there is the ubiquitous *cha chaan teng* ('tea-meal room'), a kind of inexpensive local eatery that contrasts with a proper restaurant. On this ground, it is a candidate for the dynamic equivalent of *kopitiam*. What if we were translating into Japanese instead? Here the dynamic equivalent could be the *kissaten* ('tea-drinking shop'), by virtue of the fact that it is more casual and rustic than the Western-style café. On a material level, the *kopitiam*, *cha chaan teng*, and *kissaten* are very different. The *cha chaan teng* is always air-conditioned, and waiters and waitresses are hired to serve customers; as for a *kissaten*, the tight configuration of its furniture makes it a cozier enclave than a *kopitiam*. As far as dynamic equivalence is concerned, however, these material differences are not that important, just as a kiss is sensuously a very different gesture than a handshake. The criterion, rather, is whether the candidate TL word-concept generates a response from the TL reader that is similar in nature and degree to how the typical SL reader intuitively responds to the corresponding SL word.

By establishing the *kopitiam*, *cha chaan teng*, and *kissaten* (and we can make a list of culinary institutions in other cultures with similar relative status) as dynamic equivalents, we are not suggesting that these words should automatically translate one another in every situation. If the purpose of the translation (see Chapter 3) is to convey the cultural uniqueness of the ST, dynamic equivalence would be counter-productive, as it has the effect of **acculturating** the foreign SL word-concept into the TL culture, to the extent that the TT reader may not even be aware that s/he has in fact just encountered an unfamiliar, culture-specific item. This effect is desirable in some but certainly not all cases of translation.

Hence, to signal the foreignness of *kopitiam* as a Singapore-specific culinary establishment while making sure its referential meaning is not completely lost on TT readers, we can opt for a hybrid solution that couples borrowing with an in-text commentary that builds in a dynamically equivalent component: '*kopitiam*, an inexpensive eatery in Singapore roughly equivalent to the XXX'. Here XXX is any culinary institution in the target culture deemed equal in standing to the *kopitiam*. In so doing, we are turning the translation into a *meta-translation*, that is, a translation that talks about translation ('roughly equivalent to ...'). This could still be a controversial solution, not least because it is cumbersome and produces a longer TT. But for present purposes, this hypothetical problem illustrates how translation entails more than just transporting words across pages and languages, focusing our attention on the importance of gauging the relative values of comparable entities in the SL and TL cultures.

Try this

Suppose you and your Japanese friend are visiting the residence of a mutual American acquaintance on invitation. Upon entering the doorway, your Japanese friend utters: *O-jama shimasu*. This is a Japanese politeness expression that literally means 'I'm going to disturb you'. It is often used when entering someone's personal space, serving as a kind of pre-emptive apology for intruding into that other person's space.

Now your American acquaintance asks you what your Japanese friend has just said. As you can imagine, a literal translation ('I'm going to disturb you') will create issues; depending on the tone it might even be construed as a **face-threatening act**. Try translating the Japanese utterance in two different ways as follows, and then discuss which option you prefer.

Option A: Using the idea of dynamic equivalence, translate the utterance in a way that would produce the same effect on your American host as it would on a Japanese native speaker.

Option B: Translate the utterance in a way that would retain its foreignness, making sure at the same time that it would not cause any offence to your American host.

The translator's liberty

As we can see from these examples, dynamic equivalence is concerned not so much with the text per se but with whether the text works equally well for TT readers in the context of their language and culture. As such, dynamic equivalence is also known as **functional equivalence** (Nida 1964: 171). There is indeed some similarity between Nida's theory and the functionalist paradigm, which we will be discussing in the next chapter, in the specific sense that both are oriented toward the TL culture. This is particularly so in cases where the translation bears the same purpose as its original text, for example, to convey a set of instructions, to issue a certain warning, to promote a commercial product, and so forth.

In terms of its operation, however, Nida's theory tends to be somewhat piecemeal: it works within the bounds of a relatively small unit of translation, usually a discrete expression. While the translator is not obliged to reproduce the form of the ST expression, s/he is not free to alter its informational content in a substantive way. Nida instructs that in translating a problematic text segment,

> one is not free to make in the text any and all kinds of explanatory additions and/or expansions. There is a very definite limit as to what is proper translation in this difficult area: one may make explicit in the text only what is *linguistically* implicit in the immediate context of the problematic passage.
> (Nida & Taber 1969: 111)

This is the notion of **explicitation** in translation. Explicitation is intrinsically bound: it relates to the internal structures of language and is generally, but not always, an obligatory move. In the Thai language, the informal term *faen* can mean either boyfriend/husband or girlfriend/wife. When translating into English, one might need to perform explicitation according to the specific gender referred to – what Nida describes as 'the immediate context of the problematic passage'. And after the gender is settled, the translator has to decide whether or not the couple in question is married. In the course of this explicitation, inference is necessary in order to determine the identity of the referent. For example, if a middle-aged woman uses *faen*, she probably (but not necessarily) means 'husband' rather than 'boyfriend'; it would be wise for the translator not to make any hasty assumptions, and to instead undertake due diligence in pinning down the referent based on the available contextual information.

Is this move obligatory in English translation? Not strictly, for in rendering *faen* I can still choose to use 'partner' (though slightly old-fashioned) or 'lover' (might sound too intimate for the situation). Further: consider the case where the gender of the *faen* in question is meant to be ambiguous in the ST – a real possibility in a Thai social setting where the 'third gender' is a recognised phenomenon. In this case, gender explicitation would be a wrong technique to use, and 'partner' or 'lover' would be apt, depending on the degree of intimacy required.

Try this

Can you think of other ways of getting around the gender ambiguity of the Thai word *faen* in English translation? Does your devised method fall within the limits on the translator's liberty set down by Eugene Nida?

Explicitation

This concept is a bit slippery because different authors use it to mean slightly different things. This proliferation of theoretical terms and differing senses of the same term is a classic post-Babel issue. Compare the following definitions.

Vinay and Darbelnet (1995 [1958])

'A stylistic translation technique which consists of making explicit in the target language what remains implicit in the source language because it is apparent from either the context or the situation. Excessive use leads to overtranslation' (342). For example, we may translate the English 'students' into the feminine form *les étudiantes* in French with reference to 'St Mary's School' or 'Vassar College', since these are female-only institutions (116).

Blum-Kulka (2004; first appeared in 1986)

A postulated universal tendency of translators to render the TT more cohesive than the ST. This means the degree of syntactic redundancy is higher in the TT. For example, a translator might insert more markers (e.g., subordinating conjunctions) than is absolutely necessary to overtly signal logical relations between clauses in the TL, or s/he may feel compelled to fill out an elliptical structure in the ST. This tendency is known as the **Explicitation Hypothesis**. For more on cohesion and translation, see Chapter 4 of this book.

Klaudy (2001)

A catch-all term that includes obligatory and optional moves of linguistic expansion in translation. This means as long as a piece of TL is extended within reasonable bounds of its linguistic frame, there is explicitation.

Berman (2012 [1985])

'[The] manifestation of something that is not apparent, but concealed or repressed, in the original ... [It] aims to render "clear" what does not wish to be clear in the original' (245). For Berman, explicitation is a means of clarifying the SL, and he considers that as an undesirable intervention in translation. Berman's ideas have been co-opted to fortify conceptual theories that critique domesticating tendencies in translation, particularly in the Anglo-American world (see pp.68, 164–168).

These definitions show that explicitation is variously seen as a technique (Vinay & Darbelnet), an empirical tendency in translating (Blum-Kulka; Klaudy), and a cultural trait with adverse ideological implications (Berman). What cuts across these different definitions is that explicitation relates to the structure of the language itself or at most its immediate context.

Thus, even though dynamic equivalence appears to grant the translator a degree of freedom, this freedom is spatially circumscribed, namely that the translator cannot exercise his or her will beyond the frame of a given lexical expression. This conception differs from functionalist theories of translation, where the focus is on the text as a holistic entity rather than on a particular specimen of language such as an idiom or metaphor. As we will see in the next chapter, this can justify more radical shifts beyond the level of the utterance.

Semantic vs. communicative translation

The theory of dynamic equivalence proved to be highly influential; in many ways, it constituted the foundation of contemporary translation studies, and inspired other variations on similar themes. One of these was Peter Newmark's *semantic* versus *communicative translation*, espoused in *A Textbook of Translation*. Conceptually, this pair of terms closely parallels Nida's formal versus dynamic equivalence, although Newmark's theory purports to introduce a new dimension: text function.

To Newmark, Nida's theory lays claim to universality when in fact it is based on the very specific practice of biblical translation. Newmark's premise is that translating the Bible yields a very different set of strategies and techniques than translating other genres – a recipe book, a comic strip, a contractual agreement, a novel, a presidential speech, and so on. Each of these texts carries with it a very different function and demands a different treatment in translation. More specifically, a text can serve primarily to relay factual information; to convey an author's subjective attitude or emotion; to persuade the reader into taking a particular course of action; or any combination of these. This idea of imputing varying functions to texts is not Newmark's invention; it has a German origin, and we will be covering this in greater detail under the functionalist paradigm in Chapter 3.

For now let us return to Newmark's signature concept of semantic versus communicative translation. Semantic translation 'follows the thought processes of the [ST] author, tends to over-translate, pursues nuances of meaning, yet aims at concision in order to reproduce pragmatic impact' (Newmark 1988: 47). Communicative translation, on the other hand, 'concentrates on the message and the main force of the text, tends to under-translate, to be simple, clear and brief, and is always written in a natural and resourceful style' (48). Simply, semantic translation tends toward *representing the text as it is*, though not to the rigidity of a word-for-word or phrase-for-phrase translation, while communicative translation focuses on *relaying the situation* in the text to TT readers in the most sensible and economical way.

Consider the case of phatic communion, for which different languages have different conventions. The ubiquitous 'How're you?' (not used in a literal sense – as in asking a sick person about his or her condition) in Anglophone cultures would generally work in contemporary Chinese-speaking cultures, but a more senior generation of Chinese people might prefer the question 'Have you eaten your meal?' as a means of starting a conversation. Translating this semantically into English would give us what Newmark (1988: 110) calls **referential accuracy**. But clearly in this case, the resulting translation would be ridiculous (unless that is the intended effect), because the interlocutor is not actually interested in the issue of eating meals here. Communicative translation ('How're you?' and the like) becomes the plausible solution, because it brings out what Newmark calls the **pragmatic economy** of the text (110).

Where Newmark departs from Nida is in how he encapsulates these opposite poles within a broader frame of translation methods. We may represent this idea with a scalar figure (Figure 2.1; Newmark [1988: 45] uses a 'flattened V-diagram' instead).

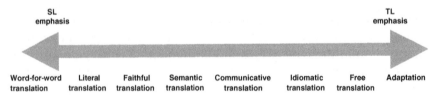

Figure 2.1 Translation as a dynamic repertoire

The strength of this model lies in its conceptualisation of translation methods as a spectrum of possibilities, a dynamic repertoire. This relativises the age-old dichotomy of literal versus free translation and its various guises, including the formal/semantic versus dynamic/communicative pairs, enabling us to appreciate translation as manifested in a wide range of textual practices. That these various methods are placed on a single cline implies that they are born equal rather than hierarchical. In this regard, Figure 2.1 represents an inclusive and democratic model that covers textual practices that are conventionally perceived as either technically trivial or altogether alien to the purview of translation studies.

Thus, on one extreme end of the scale, we have word-for-word translation, which is an impossible strategy in many cases, but which nonetheless has applications in restricted contexts, such as the glossing of foreign terms to deliberately foreground their origination in a different culture. This would come in useful, for instance, in ethnographic writing, which involves the translation of terms from less familiar SL cultures for TL readers. On the other end of the continuum is adaptation, as in the transposition of a novel for the stage. Some decades ago this would hardly be considered translation except in a far-fetched, figurative sense; but today it is very much an integral part of translation studies. This is evidenced in the fact that adaptation is given an independent entry in at least two major reference books in the field, namely *Routledge Encyclopedia of Translation Studies* (Baker & Saldanha 2009) and *Handbook of Translation Studies* (Gambier & van Doorslaer 2010).

Adaptation

Adaptation is another tricky term in translation studies. We have seen from Table 2.2 that it is a procedure where a situation described by the SL turns into a new situation in the TL. Yet the term is also used to describe a change of mode and medium that transpires, say, when Shakespeare's *Hamlet* is turned into a film, either with or without a change in the language (but remember in this context that turning Shakespearean English into modern-day English counts as intralingual translation). The term is also sometimes used loosely to describe any radical changes made to a ST in the course of translation, and can lapse into what is called **appropriation** (Sanders 2016).

The philosopher Slavoj Žižek has a very interesting take on this. In explaining his approach in 'retelling' the Greek play *Antigone* by Sophocles, Žižek (2016) critiques the idea of fidelity or faithfulness to the form of a classic work, advocating that we 'treat [the work] as "open", pointing towards the future' (xii), in other words, to adapt the work to fit with our contemporary condition. Although Žižek does not expressly see himself as a translator, his observations are very relevant to the idea of translation as a dynamic repertoire, although it is important to note that he is not looking at particular expressions but at the text as a whole. Particularly worth reading is Žižek's formulation on the dialectic between faithfulness and betrayal in respect of rendering a classic for a contemporary readership:

> This is how we should approach numerous recent attempts to stage some classical opera by not only transposing its action into a different (most often contemporary) era, but also by changing some basic facts of the narrative itself. There is no a priori abstract criterion which would allow us to judge the success or failure: each such intervention is a risky act and must be judged by its own immanent standards. Such experiments often ridiculously misfire – however, not always, and there is no way to tell it in advance, so one has to take the risk. Only one thing is sure: *the only way to be faithful to a classic work is to take such a risk* – avoiding it, *sticking to the traditional letter*, is the safest way to *betray the spirit* of the classic. (Žižek 2016: xii; emphasis added)

Note that Žižek is referring specifically to the retelling of ancient classics, where there is a huge temporal gap to be traversed; whether his observations should apply to the adaptation of contemporary works is a matter of debate.

Within Newmark's scheme, semantic and communicative translation can be said to represent the two core methods: the pro-SL and pro-TL poles respectively, around which the other methods revolve. Although Newmark provides definitions for each of the methods on his scale (Newmark 1988: 45–47), their relative position on the scale is rather more important than their precise meaning. Thus, even though we are told that faithful translation 'attempts to reproduce the precise contextual meaning of the original within the constraints of the TL grammatical structures', whereas semantic translation differs from this 'only in as far as it must take more account of the aesthetic value … of the SL text' (46), in actual practice it would be difficult to draw a clear boundary between the two.

Nor is it necessary to draw such boundaries, which will always be artificial. Our main take-away from Newmark's scale is the general sense that we can slide from one point to another, which means we are not locked into one method of translating, and we are certainly not obliged to subscribe to the zero-sum game of 'literal' versus 'free' translation. Rather, we can have the best of both worlds, and even go beyond these categories to see translating as a fluid practice. In determining how to translate, a translator can consciously choose to position himself or herself at some point on the scale, and that is contingent on several factors, including the type of text s/he is dealing with as well as the projected purpose of the translation task (more on this in Chapter 3). Even when dealing with a single text, a translator may need to keep adjusting his position along the scale in treating different segments of the text. Metaphors, for example, may require different strategies in their translation. Some stock metaphors in the SL may find TL equivalents with corresponding images, in which case semantic translation may be applied. More culture-specific metaphors, however, may need to be replaced by a TL metaphor with approximately the same meaning, or otherwise be paraphrased. A text containing metaphors of different kinds may thus require the translator to constantly shuttle among various points on the scale. Of course, these decisions are not made at the whim of the translator, but are contingent on the nature of the text being translated and the importance of the metaphor to the meaning of the utterance in question.

Let us now look at an actual instance of communicative translation at work. A NHK documentary takes its camera to an old vending machine that dispenses hot noodles in a remote part of Japan. It is cold winter. A Japanese man is eating a bowl of hot noodles he has bought from the vending machine. The man is a truck driver and has stopped by briefly in the middle of a long journey to take a quick lunch. After finishing his noodles, he says to the camera: *Ganbarimasu* and sets off to work again. The Japanese word literally means '(I'll) work hard' or '(I'll) do my best', and in most cases would be translated as such.

Six ways to translate metaphors

Newmark (1988: 106–113) proposes six procedures for translating metaphors depending on their type. This constitutes yet another spectrum – from 'dead' to 'original'.

1. **Dead** metaphors: Metaphors whose images are not consciously invoked. Some dead metaphors can be translated literally, while others find convenient and conventional substitutes in the TL. For example, for the phrase 'the field of human knowledge', French has *domaine* or *sphere* for 'field', while 'at the bottom of the hill' can be rendered as *au fond de la colline*.

2. **Cliché** metaphors: Metaphors that have become banal, e.g., 'not a *backwater* but a *breakthrough* in educational development', 'a *jewel in the crown* of the country's education', etc. In authoritative texts such as political speeches, these must be retained (*mare stagnante, percée*, etc.); in anonymous, informative texts, these clichés can be reduced to sense, e.g., 'use up every ounce of energy' → *tendre ses dernières énergies*, or reduced to dead metaphor: 'rapier-like wit' → *esprit mordant*.

3. **Stock** (or standard) metaphors: Metaphors that are established and exude 'a certain emotional warmth', but not yet overused. They can be translated by retaining the same image if they have equal currency in the TL, e.g., 'keep the pot boiling' → *faire bouillir la marmite*; 'wooden face' → *hölzernes Gesicht*. If the image does not work in the TL, replace it with one that is equally unmarked within the TL register: 'that upset the applecart' → *das hat alles über den Haufen geworfen*. Other methods include reducing to sense, and retaining the metaphor plus adding the sense, e.g., *il a une mémoire d'éléphant* → 'He never forgets – like an elephant'.

4. **Adapted** metaphors: Stock metaphors with slight alterations. These should be translated into another metaphor that works just as well in the TL, e.g., 'the ball is a little in their court' → *c'est peut-être à eux de jouer*. The alternative is to reduce the metaphor to sense, e.g., 'get them in the door' → *les introduire*.

5. **Recent** metaphors: A metaphorical neologism, which can either be a new metaphor designating a quality or object, or a metaphor designating a new object or process. These can be translated by borrowing or calquing the SL term. Obviously recent metaphors become clichéd with the passing of time. Newmark's examples of 'in' or 'with it' (translated as dans *le vent*) as metaphors for 'fashionable' and the then neologism of 'head-hunting' (calqued as *chasse aux têtes*) are by now clichéd. 'Walkman', which Newmark recommends translating as *transistor portaif* (as a way of 'decommercialising' the product), is now completely obsolete.

6. **Original** metaphors: Creative metaphors with poetic value. In authoritative and expressive texts, these metaphors 'contain the core of an important writer's message, his personality, his comment on life', and thus should be 'transferred neat', i.e.,

their images should be retained, even if there exist cultural equivalents in the TL. In anonymous, non-literary texts, these metaphors may be retained to sustain readers' interest in the foreignness of the expressions. But they can be modified or reduced to sense if the metaphor is inconsistent with the TT style. Metaphors deemed obscure or unimportant may be reduced to sense, e.g., 'Oxford, a place in Lyonnesse' (Evelyn Waugh) → 'Oxford, lost in the mythology of a remote, vanished region.'

Watch this clip

The documentary, entitled 'A Taste of Home', under the NHK series *Document 72 Hours*, can be found at www.youtube.com/watch?v=nb1W-NfH1u4. For the particular expression discussed here, see the segment 00:23:11 – 00:24:10.

The NHK English subtitler(s) avoids the obvious and goes for a different and somewhat surprising option: 'Fully recharged'. How do we make sense of this translation? '(I'll) work hard' and '(I'll) try my best' are semantic translations; they adhere to the dictionary sense of the Japanese word and strive for referential accuracy. 'Fully recharged', on the other hand, does not work on the level of semantics at all. We know this because if we **back-translate** this phrase, which means translating it in reverse order from the TL into the SL, we would derive a very different Japanese expression than *Ganbarimasu*.

The back-translation test

Back-translation can be used as a mechanism for checking the accuracy of a piece of translation. The method is simple. First, after completing a translation, translate the TT into the SL, as if the TT were an original text. Then, compare this translation (now in the SL) with the ST. Finally, note down any discrepancies between the two texts, and check the TT for possible errors with reference to the ST.

Note, however, that the back-translation test is handy only for relatively close translations, i.e., when the translator is operating on the left side of the Newmark spectrum (Figure 2.1). It is much less functional as far as communicative translation and other strategies on the right side of the spectrum are concerned, as technical accuracy, in the sense of close correspondence to the ST, is not the object of those strategies. The test thus works best for word-to-word translation, and gradually weakens as we move toward adaption.

A back-translation test presumes symmetry between the ST and TT; following Pym (2014: 6) we may call this **natural equivalence**. But oftentimes the ST and TT are asymmetric – translating from Language A into Language B does not give rise to the same textual outcome as translating in the other direction. This latter type of relation is what Pym calls **directional equivalence** (24). In our NHK example, the given subtitle operates on the conversational situation of the utterance rather than the linguistic contour of the utterance itself. Recall that the truck driver is having a well-deserved lunch in a cold weather before resuming his work, so the question to ask here is this: what is the truck driver really trying to say with *Ganbarimasu* in this setting? We might venture an answer like this: 'This bowl of noodles has filled me and I'm now ready to start driving again'. 'I'll work hard' and 'I'll do my best' are acceptable insofar as they relate to the fact that the man is back to his work again, but both of these expressions divorce the man's utterance from the noodles he has just eaten. They also sound a bit like a promise to the viewer that the truck driver will do his best at work, which is a little awkward in English communication, though completely natural in Japanese. It is almost like an English speaker saying 'All the best!' to himself or herself. English viewers would probably not respond to 'I'll work hard' in the same way as Japanese viewers would to *Ganbarimasu* – recall the centrality of the response of TT readers in dynamic equivalence; the same idea works here.

In this scenario, the most natural and pragmatically equivalent English expression to use would probably be 'See you around' or something similar. And while 'See you around' is a possible translation, 'fully recharged' goes one step further. It ties *Ganbarimasu* to the material situation that produces it and dynamically interprets the word within its pragmatic economy, hence producing a piece of communicative translation 'in a natural and resourceful style' (Newmark 1988: 48).

(Un)translatability and its discontents

The theories covered so far constitute the equivalence paradigm by virtue of their insistence on finding linguistic-level correspondences between a given ST and a matching TT. The unit of translation that is operative in these theories is intra-sentential: the word, phrase, clause, and sentence. The paradigm has immense implications for practical translating at a technical level, providing us with a framework encompassing both global strategies (formal/semantic versus dynamic/communicative translation) and microtextual techniques of linguistic transfer (Catford's and also Vinay & Darbelnet's schemata).

In considering equivalence, we must come face to face with the corollary notion of **untranslatability**. In translation studies, untranslatability almost has the status of a vulgar word; it is seen as the nemesis of translation, the ultimate evil to be conquered. That is in a way understandable, for the translation profession takes great pride in overcoming the linguistic and cultural issues that arise in the course of effectively communicating a ST to its TL readers. But it is one thing to recognise and acknowledge the fact of untranslatability, and quite another to dwell in and lament on it. There is an abundance of scholarly literature that adopts the latter attitude, giving loads of examples to tell us why translation is never going to work out perfectly.

But no one ever said translation was going to work out perfectly; and imperfection does not stop translation from performing its function in the real world. Not only is such scholarly discourse wholly unproductive – it does not tell us what to do in the face of untranslatability except to resign to our fate with a lot of regret; it also implicitly registers the attitude that languages and cultures are somehow to be made contiguous through translation. At first that might seem to be a most logical position to take from the vantage point of translating, but it is in fact potentially pernicious. In its extreme form, this mentality that translation should serve as a panacea to eradicate differences and fill (all) gaps works to efface what Pym (2014) describes (with reference to Heidegger) as 'the productive conflict of differences' (94) between languages and cultures. If indeed the conflict of differences can be productive – and of course there will be times it can be destructive – it follows that we should acknowledge at least a measure of inherent incommensurability between languages and cultures, allow some gaps to be left unfilled, and put untranslatability in perspective.

So as we appreciate the practical usefulness of equivalence theories, let us consider the counterintuitive idea that untranslatability might be of some value to understanding the nature of intercultural communication. Our working definition of untranslatability is this:

Untranslatability

Any situation where an element in the SL text or SL culture cannot be rendered in the TL completely and/or economically.

An untranslatable 'element' can take various forms. Earlier we discussed semantic gaps, where a word-concept exists in one language but not in another; that constitutes a source of untranslatability at a lexical level, although this can be partially mitigated by way of borrowing plus explicitation or extended commentary. An untranslatable element can also be something less discrete, such as a grammatical-pragmatic meaning that permeates a stretch of discourse. Japanese provides us with some exemplars here:

Dialogue 1

Tanaka:	Sensei, ashita-no kaigi-ni irasshaimasuka?
	'Professor, are you going to the conference tomorrow?'
Professor:	Ee, ikimasu. Tanaka-kun-wa?
	'Yes, I'm going. How about you, Tanaka?'
Tanaka:	Hai, watashi-mo mairimasu.
	'Yes, I'm going too.'

Dialogue 2

Tanaka:	Sensei, hisho-ni sono hon-no namae-o o-kiki-ni narimasu ka.
	'Professor, are you going to ask the secretary the name of that book?'
Professor:	Iie, kiki-masen.
	'No, (I'm) not going to ask.'
Tanaka:	Jaa, watashi ga o-kiki-shimasu.
	'Then, I will ask (her).'

(Adapted from Tsujimura 2014: 412–413
with minor edits)

In Dialogue 1, three Japanese verbs meaning 'to go' are used, namely *irrasshaimasu*, *ikimasu*, and *mairimasu*. Japanese pragmatics dictates that extra-textual factors, in this case the relative status of the interlocutors, have a crucial bearing on lexical choice in conversation. Here we have the student Tanaka speaking to his professor, and the need to express respectfulness motivates Tanaka's use of the honorific form *irrasshaimasu* (comprising the honorific expression *irrassharu* and the polite copular – *masu*); this contrasts with the polite form *ikimasu* used by the professor in response to Tanaka's question. A further contrast appears in Tanaka's next turn, where he uses the humble form *mairimasu* to refer to his intention to attend the conference. Social distance is lexicalised in the three words that carry the same referential meaning. As the translations in the dialogue show, there is no way we can reproduce this pragmatic nuance in English in an economical way: the same English verb ('going') is used to translate the three Japanese verbs. Of course we can tackle this by way of a footnote commentary, but that hardly qualifies as economical.

Similarly, in Dialogue 2 we see the recurring verb 'to ask' (and its negation) in different formations: *o-kiki-ni narimasu* (honorific), *kiki-masen* (polite), and *o-kiki-shimasu* (humble). Once again, Tanaka uses the honorific when addressing his professor, who is socially superior – *o* being the Japanese honorific marker and *ni narimasu* ('to become') a grammatical pattern that can be turned into a politeness formula. Literally, the clause from Tanaka's first utterance reads: 'Will (your act of) asking be realised?' The professor replies in the polite *masen* form. As with *ikimasu* in Dialogue 1, the form *kikimasen* also signals professional distance, as the polite form stands in contrast to the casual form *kikanai* ('to not ask'); if the professor had used the casual form here instead, that would indicate that he and Tanaka are on familiar terms. Lastly, Tanaka uses the humble form of the same verb in his next turn, activating the honorific pattern *o…shimasu* ('to do…'); it reads literally: '[I will] do the act of asking' (cf. the polite form of the same reply *kikimasu* ('[I will] ask'). The English translation flattens the three variants of 'to ask'; it cannot do otherwise, which shows that the pragmatic subtleties, which are embedded in the SL grammar, are not entirely reproducible.

What we have here is a classic case where the distinctive character of a language is embodied in its very fabric – the source of a translator's nightmare. At this point we can choose to throw our hands in the air and grudgingly declare that the above dialogues are impossible specimens of text for nuanced translation. This response, however, belies the assumption that the specificity of Japanese grammar is something that *must be resolved* for the English speaker; in other words, it is a barrier that obstructs what should otherwise be an instance of unimpeded crosscultural communication.

But what if we were to take a step back and ask: should those intricacies of Japanese politeness even be communicable in English or any other language? Must they be so eminently translatable? Or can we accept untranslatability as it is; that is to say: to see it not as a problem as such but as a portal through which we can enter into and come out from another linguistic world? This latter world could encapsulate a reality that is different from that which we are familiar with, and therefore create fruitful tension with our habitual modes of thought and ways of behaviour. It can compel us to consider the possibility that all our conventionalised modes and ways are less than universal, thereby prompting us to adopt a more relativist, less parochial attitude toward other languages and cultures. This argument affiliates with the **Sapir-Whorf hypothesis**, also known as the linguistic relativity theory. The basic premise of this theory is that languages reflect different worldviews, and there are strong and weak versions of it. Without taking the extreme stance that languages are so radically different as to be isolated islands, we can say with some conviction that any given language must be allowed to retain its own idiosyncrasies, and therefore an element of untranslatability.

So in respect of the Japanese examples above, they are as they are. The point is to let the recalcitrant elements *be*, and keep in check this obsession to translate into, so as to understand in, one's own terms. There should be no compulsion to render them fully or economically into English or any other language. Perfect translatability need not be the default or only desirable outcome in communication across languages and cultures. This claim does not preclude the possibility of crosslingual and crosscultural communication for most practical purposes; in fact, it affords significance to such an enterprise. In their book *Metrolingualism*, Pennycook and Otsuji (2015) propose that we steer away from the assumption that a common linguistic denominator must exist to facilitate communication between persons speaking different mother tongues: 'The argument that we all need to share one language in order to get by needs to be seen as a very particular language ideology that assumes that linguistic diversity can only be overcome through a shared language' (69). Instead it is completely possible for different language resources to be deployed simultaneously and spontaneously to fulfil contingent communicative demands in concrete settings (such as markets and restaurant kitchens). In these situations, untranslatability becomes a non-issue.

Imagine the scenario where all languages can be immaculately transposed into one another: this brings us close to a pre-Babelian world marked by the absence of language barriers (cf. the story of Babel excerpted at the end of Chapter 1). At first, and probably to many people, this might sound wonderful, but in actuality, where we might gain in terms of communicative convenience, we inevitably lose out in terms of the value of difference – or 'the productive conflict of differences', to cite Pym again – that languages bestow upon us. After all, there is no point in there being different languages when there isn't a degree of difficulty in communicating across them; in other words: how is Japanese *Japanese* and English *English* if we were able to translate every single nuance, every linguistic nook and cranny, of the one into the other?

On this view, the vision of total translatability, or perfect equivalence, is almost nightmarish, as it entails each language relinquishing its identity in the name of a utopian communality unhindered by linguistic barriers. And if the prospect of total translatability were realised, language acquisition (TESOL, TEFL, etc.) would probably cease to be a very interesting field. This is because the best experience one can gain from learning a foreign language is really to become acquainted with – and frustrated by – the untranslatable, and it is in this connection that translation has traditionally been associated with the field of applied linguistics. To work through a translation exercise in a foreign language classroom (even mentally) does not mean to embattle and finally conquer the linguistic Other through translation; it means to encounter, interface with, and ideally enter into this linguistic Other, to seek a channel of communication while embracing all the differences between Us and Them. In the final analysis, translation negotiates linguistic heterogeneity but does not, cannot, and must not obliterate it.

This is where **crosscultural** communication can lapse into **intercultural** communication: instead of merely crossing, or translating across, language boundaries, we dynamically interact with another language and culture more intricately and intimately. We do not just *know* the dictionary meaning of a foreign term; we *go there*, even if just virtually, and experience for ourselves how it is what it is. And what comes after this is **transcultural** communication where, by virtue of translation, each culture transforms and enriches itself by absorbing aspects of the other.

Further reading and reflection

1. Read Chapter 7 of Peter Newmark's *A Textbook of Translation* (Newmark 1988). Nida's dynamic equivalence and Newmark's communicative translation are very attractive strategies of translating, because they empower the translator to render the ST flexibly, creatively, and even imaginatively, as opposed to remaining subservient to the ST. Do you think dynamic equivalence and communicative translation are *always* superior to formal equivalence and semantic translation respectively? Based on what you have read, can you come up with your own examples where we should *not* translate dynamically and communicatively?

2. Read an article titled 'Translation as Intercultural Communication' by Martha Cheung (2014). The following is a short extract from the article (p.181; emphasis added) describing four kinds of translational interaction in an intercultural setting.

---

1. Interaction that is manifested in the form of **assimilation**, defined by ICS [Intercultural Communication Studies] researchers as referring to the process of change undergone by individuals – to the extent of not maintaining their native cultural identity – in order to conform to the expected norms of the mainstream culture, or, where immigrants are concerned, the host culture. This type of interaction occurs in works of translation, too, for they also undergo a process of change – sometimes to the extent of not maintaining the cultural distinctness of the source text – in order to conform to the expected norms of the host culture. These are domesticating translations that, wittingly or unwittingly, result in the erasure of difference.

2. Interaction that manifests itself in **cultural convergence**, which refers in ICS to how people of different cultural backgrounds manage to meet at a point where more mutual understanding can be attained, and, in translation studies, to the productive hybridity of translated texts that would lead to enhanced crosscultural understanding and the enrichment of (the language of) one culture by another.

3. Interaction that takes the form of what ICS researchers call **adaptation**, which involves change to suit a new situation, often in purpose-related encounters, and between communicators of unequal power relations. In TS [Translation Studies] such interactions are often accented as subversion, and/or as deliberate and triumphant miscommunication. They are observable in translations undertaken in situations of unequal power relations, and especially if the host culture has been forced to undertake the task.

---

4. Interaction that takes the form of **separation**. In ICS this refers to the rejection of the possibility of common bonds with dominant group members, while in TS such interaction is shown in works of translation or in interpreting activities that resist, via the strategy of foreignization, the imposition of one set of values by one culture on another. And, just as separation would result in (self-) alienation, foreignizing translations would lead to various degree of self-exoticization or exoticization of one culture by another.

Can you think of one example each for assimilation, cultural convergence, adaptation, and separation, as described below? Your examples could be based on your own experience in interacting with people from different languages and cultures, or they could be drawn from other sources you have come into contact with, such as travel accounts or fiction.

3. Read a short section on the concept of transculturation from the book *Enlarging Translation, Empowering Translators* by Maria Tymoczko (2014: 120–127). According to the author, transculturation has the following features:

1. It 'includes such things as the transmission and uptake of beliefs and practices related to religion, social organization, and government from one people to another, as well as the spread of artistic forms, including music, the visual arts, literary forms, and even tale types. The concept of transculturation covers many aspects of material culture: the uptake of technology and tools, agricultural practices, clothing, food, housing, transportation, and more recent cultural domains related to the modern media. The popularity of Chinese and Mexican food, reggae music, and Japanese anime in the United States are examples of transculturation' (120).

2. It 'requires the *performance* of the borrowed cultural forms in the receptor environment. When transculturation is operative, forms from one culture are appropriated by another and integrated with previous practices, beliefs, values, and knowledge. They become part of the life ways of those on the receiving end of transculturation. This is the significance of the OED [*Oxford English Dictionary*] definition of transculturation as *acculturation*. In textual domains transculturation often involves transposing elements that constitute the overcodings of a text, including elements of a literary system (poetics, genres, tale types, and other formal literary elements); textual technologies including literacy, printing,

and electronic media have also been transculturated. Elements expressed in or carried by language can also be transculturated, such as discourses and world-views. Such elements then become part of the performative repertory in the receiving culture's speech, literature, music, politics, economic system, religion, and so forth' (121).

3. It 'does not necessarily entail representation as a component of the process of cultural uptake. In some cases of transculturation, the dimension of represen-tation may be so minimal as to be essentially nil ... That is, the form may have become so completely naturalized in the receptor culture that it is not seen as "other" or as being representative of the source culture in any way. The transcul-turation may also have proceeded in such a way as to obscure the point of origin of the cultural element, or the transculturated practice may even come with an incorrect attribution. Pizza is an example of cultural uptake of this latter sort in much of the world: it is often not experienced as specifically Italian at all nor does it stand as a representation of anything Italian to the (literal) consumer as it does in the United States' (121).

Based on this and the previous reading, do you think there is a substantive difference among the crosscultural, the intercultural, and the transcultural as far as communication between different peoples is concerned? How is the role of translation different in each of these modalities of communication?

Topic Map

TEXT-TYPE THEORY

- Key author: Katharina Reiss (1923–)
- Representative work: 'Text-types, Translation Types and Translation assessment'
- Theory/model: A text may be informative, expressive, or operative depending on its dominant function. For informative texts, the translator's focus is on the *message*; minor-to-moderate alteration of ST form is permitted; for expressive texts, the translator's focus is on ST *form*, of which there should be no or minimal alteration; for operative texts, the translator's focus is on the *effect*; moderate-to-major alteration of ST form is possible if deemed necessary to produce desired effect on TT receiver.

TRANSLATORIAL ACTION

- Key author: Justa Holz-Mänttäri (1936–)
- Representative work: *Translatorisches Handeln* (Translatorial Action)
- Theory/model: Translation, conceptualised as translatorial action, is a process of delivering a text or some other mode of intercultural mediation such as professional consultancy; it is embedded within a larger communicative event to actively facilitate cooperation between parties situated in different languages and cultures.

SKOPOS THEORY

purpose

- Key authors: Hans J. Vermeer (1930–2010) and Katharina Reiss (1923–)
- Representative work: 'Skopos and Commission in Translational Action'; *Towards a General Theory of Translational Action*
- Theory/model: A translation is determined by its skopos, or purpose. How a text is to be translated depends on the goal of the action and the specific requirements of the translation commission.

LOCALISATION

- Key author: Anthony Pym (1956–)
- Representative work: *The Moving Text*
- Theory/model: As a product or service disseminates from one locale to another, it adapts itself to the linguistic and cultural frame of the receiving market. This process entails textual translation and semiotic transfiguration.

The uses and users of text

Function is an instrumentalist notion, and has been a central preoccupation in contemporary translation studies since the very beginning. This is completely unsurprising, given the applied nature of the subject matter at hand. An emphasis on function means our primary concern lies with how texts, and this includes translated texts, are actually read and used. By now this should not sound unfamiliar; as we saw in the previous chapter, Eugene Nida's signature theory is that of dynamic equivalence, otherwise known as functional equivalence. As for Peter Newmark, his brand of communicative translation is basically a functionalist one, seeking to more or less assimilate the ST into the reception context of the TT by taking into account TL linguistic and cultural conventions.

But functionalism in the theories of Nida and Newmark operates at the level of discrete segments of language. At its core, this strand of functionalism is linguistics-based and microtextual; it is concerned with lateral transfer between languages, even when context is taken into consideration. For example, if we decide to replace an SL idiom with a different idiom in the TL so as not to strain the TT reader, we can be said to be exercising a functionalist criterion. This type of functionalism is more concerned with the immediate response of the target reader to a given structure or expression than with how the translated text as an organic entity works toward a specific purpose. Although functionalist theories can also be about how individual words and phrases are translated, the ultimate focal point is on whether and how the text communicates meaning as a whole.

But isn't a text just made up of individual words and phrases anyway? Yes, technically; but when it comes to communication, a text is not necessarily the summation of its parts. A slogan, for example, is a piece of text on its own; and in most cases, this text constitutes a phrase or a clause. *Impossible Is Nothing* (Adidas) is a clause on the level of language: it has a grammar; it follows the subject-copular-complement structure. It is probably safe to say that the clause itself, that is to say the linguistic construction, is quite translatable, even given the fact that it reverses a conventional word order for rhetorical effect.

But when we speak of writing or translating a slogan we are speaking at the level of the text as an instance of communication, not language per se. A slogan, and its translation where applicable, is commissioned to sell a commodity; there is a defined purpose behind the language, and it is this purpose, not strictly the language, that is to be communicated. Hence, a 'straight' translation of the Adidas clause that works at the level of language (i.e., it is grammatical and sensible) may or may not give us the optimum translation of the slogan as a piece of communication. The objective test here is whether the translated slogan sufficiently appeals to prospective Adidas customers in the foreign market to make them want to buy the product advertised. *naturally accompanying*

In the Adidas example, the clause and the slogan operate at two different levels concomitantly and are conflated into one piece of language – though strictly speaking, the slogan is more **semiotic** than linguistic; it is a **sign** that also involves the nonverbal element of visual design. There is therefore a distinction between functionalism at the level of language and functionalism at the level of communication. It is the latter type of functionalism that we turn to in this chapter. Primarily advocated by German theorists, this type of functionalism has given rise to very useful theories that help us explain translational phenomena that fall outside the purview of the equivalence paradigm.

In the equivalence paradigm, the TT is the end to be arrived at; in the functionalist paradigm, it is the means to an end. Functionalist theories are *outcome-driven*: to achieve the desired end result, they are ready to manipulate the language of the ST, though they need not always do so. Note that this does not mean the functionalist paradigm encourages us to alter the ST in any way we want – as the case may be, if a literal translation best achieves the expected outcome, then that would be the optimum choice.

We may thus characterise the functionalist paradigm as opportunistic, in the sense that it offers us flexible models with which we can engage the ST. We may strictly adhere to the wording of the ST, adapt it mildly to suit TL conventions, or completely subvert it and invent a new formulation. Each of these is a valid strategy so long as the end product fulfils the expected outcome: again, the end justifies the means. Because of this orientation, even though functionalist theories are often proposed as general theories of translation with a wide applicability, they are most amenable to commercially driven situations, and it is in these situations that they best demonstrate their potential and differentiate themselves from the equivalence theories.

Text-type theory

The first important theory under the functionalist paradigm is text-type theory, espoused by Katharina Reiss. Rather than units or levels of text, this theory deals with broad textual categories and how to approach them as a whole in translation. The concept of text type has been attributed to the German linguist Karl Bühler's typology of language functions, which stipulates that different texts perform different roles in the real world, namely, informative, expressive, and appellative. On this basis, Reiss proposes three types of text in her seminal article 'Text-types, Translation Types and Translation Assessment' (Reiss 1989 [1977]). We summarise, with our own examples, Reiss's three categories as follows:

1. **Informative texts** seek to represent more or less objective facts in the real world; here, the message being conveyed, or the 'thing' external to the text that is being referred to, is the centre of focus. Exemplars of this text type include a tourist guidebook that provides essential travel information about places of interest or the programme schedule of a TV channel.
2. **Expressive texts** embody the views, attitudes, and emotions of their authors; whereas an informative text can be seen as centrifugal, pointing as it does to the outside world, an expressive text is essentially centripetal, turning instead toward authorial intent as inscribed within the formal structures of the text. Literary works, particularly poetry, are the prototype of expressive texts.
3. **Operative texts** point neither toward the real world nor toward the author, but rather toward the audience; this type of text is appellative in that it appeals to the sensibilities of the text receiver so as to elicit some desired response from this receiver, for example, to change his/her political affiliation or religious belief, or to prompt him/her to purchase a particular product or service. Commercial advertisements embody the archetypal features of an operative text.

It is important to note that there is no hard-and-fast boundary separating the three text categories; indeed, any specimen of text will probably carry the strain of more than one text type. A magazine article listing the most luxurious holiday resorts in the world (informative) implicitly persuades the reader to aspire to a jet-set lifestyle (operative). A political rally speech aims to elicit support from prospective voters (operative) through emotive rhetoric (expressive). Brochures for tourists necessarily provide objective facts about places of interests, such as opening hours, main features, and so forth (informative), but they are also operative in seeking to induce interest and attract patronage. A bilingual (English–Chinese) monthly newsletter on places of interests in Tokyo, for instance, changes dollar prices in the original text into the renminbi currency to accommodate tourists from the Chinese mainland. Tourism bureaus of major destinations come up with catchy taglines that are printed on information brochures, for example: *Austria – Arrive and Revive; Lithuania. Real is beautiful.* While a brochure may be primarily informative, the tagline that comes with it borders on the expressive.

Strictly speaking, then, every text we encounter is a functional hybrid and so we can really only speak of a text as being *primarily* informative, expressive, or operative. And even so, we will still encounter recalcitrant texts that seem to have a bit of everything and all of nothing. It is thus important to know that Reiss's tripartite model is static while texts are dynamic. While the model helps delineate core features of each text category, one must refrain from pigeonholing texts into the model. A great deal of discretion and flexibility is required on the part of the translator in responding to the functional circumstances of the task at hand.

A visual representation of Reiss's theory takes the form of an equilateral triangle, where 'informative', 'expressive', and 'operative' each occupies one vertex, and various kinds of text are distributed throughout the interior of the triangle depending on their degree of affiliation to each of the three text categories. Thus a Facebook post on a recent social event could be placed somewhere between 'informative' and 'operative', for it aims to attract attention (and 'Like' clicks) at the same time as it communicates facts. A tabloid article, on the other hand, would find itself divided between 'expressive' and 'informative', because objective information about celebrities, politicians, and so on is likely to be couched in sensational rhetoric, particularly in the headlines. As discussed above there are cases where the nature of a text can be ambivalent. An electoral speech, mentioned briefly above, stands between the expressive and the operative; but in cases where a political candidate relies heavily on objective information such as demographic data or economic figures, it can nudge toward the informative vertex, leaving the text stranded in the middle of our text-type triangle.

So how does this knowledge about different types of text help us in translation? The answer is that it provides a convenient if somewhat simplistic frame for quality assessment. Reiss (1989 [1977]: 109) postulates that a translation may be deemed successful if:

1. in an informative text it guarantees direct and full access to the conceptual content of the SL text;
2. in an expressive text it transmits a direct impression of the artistic form of the conceptual content; and
3. in an operative text it produces a text-form which will directly elicit the desired response.

In terms of translation strategy, we could further extrapolate the following principles from Reiss's criteria:

Principle 1
In translating informative texts, the translator's focus is on the *message* or *content*; this means that form (including style) is a secondary concern. Minor-to-moderate adjustments to the ST form are permissible, even desirable in cases where a literal transfer could lead to miscomprehension. For example, historical monuments often come with display boards that tell us about their significance to the place in which they are located. Such discourse sets out to inform rather than express or persuade, so a flexible translation approach is recommended – for example, SL sentence structures need not be closely attended to; repetitive material may be truncated, and so forth, provided that all the key information is retained.

Note, however, that there are important exceptions: there are certain kinds of informative text, such as corporate financial documents, that are legally binding; for example, companies that seek to be listed in the stock market need to produce formal documents detailing their financial status for the initial public offering of their shares. For such documents a translator may not tamper with the form of the text.

Principle 2
In translating expressive texts, the translator's focus is on the form, which broadly refers to the linguistic manifestation of what the author wants to say. As far as poems are concerned, a translator has minimal space for manoeuvre or manipulation at the level of form. Even a highly charged political speech needs to be treated with absolute care, as the rhetorical turns used by the speaker may embody his/her thoughts in dramatic

fashion and must be rendered closely to preserve the intended emotive impact. A prominent example that comes to mind is Martin Luther King's 'I Have A Dream', a famous speech laden with rich metaphors and impressive turns of phrase, all of which will need to be carefully addressed in the translation.

Principle 3

In translating operative texts, the translator's focus is on the *effect*. Moderate-to-major alteration of the ST form is permissible. In extreme cases the ST can be entirely rewritten, if this is reasonably deemed to be the best way to produce the desired effect on the target receiver. This 'effect' is not restricted to that which takes place 'inside' the reader's mind; it can be something more corporeal, such as clicking a button to purchase an item online, or putting a vote into the ballot box. We can therefore see an operative text as a kind of speech act, whereby what is being said (the text) is aimed at eliciting some course of action on the part of the receiver. For the translator the rule of thumb is this: the end (intended effect) justifies the means (how to translate).

For example, a sign placed in the hallway of a Japanese shopping mall reads: *koko yori saki wa, OFFICE de gozaimasu* – literally 'it is office (area) beyond this point'. Considering that this is a piece of operative text that seeks to regulate the movement of patrons, that is, to stop them from inadvertently entering office premises, an effective English translation would abandon the form and go straight for the perlocutionary effect in line with the discursive convention of English: 'Staff Only' or 'No Unauthorised Entry'.

Try this

Read and listen to Martin Luther King Jr.'s famous speech 'I Have A Dream' on the American Rhetoric website: www.americanrhetoric.com/speeches/mlkihave adream.htm

1. Find a translated version of the speech in a language of your choice on the internet. Compare the ST and TT, with special emphasis on: (1) metaphors (e.g., 'the life of the Negro is still sadly crippled by the *manacles* of segregation and the *chains* of discrimination'); (2) at least one other feature of rhetorical style (e.g., repetition of 'One hundred years later' and 'I have a dream').
2. Following text-type theory, how might you assess the quality of the translation?

With text-type theory we have in hand a user-friendly guide to orient our initial approach to translation holistically: where should my focus be in translating this particular kind of text? What textual strategy should I use in line with this focus? Should I adhere to the ST form closely, or can I recast the same message in a different form that appeals to TL readers? Should I come up with something entirely different so as to fulfil the purpose of the translation?

The last question above need not be restricted to operative texts alone; in the functionalist view, the idea of purpose dictates the entire communicative event, of which translation is a part. We tend to translate a poem closely because the purpose of translating it is to enable TL readers to appreciate its formal artistry, the subtle niceties of its language; this purpose alone justifies the use of a literal approach, simply because deviating even slightly from the form of the ST could mean altering the style of the author. On the other hand, the function of warning signs is to stop someone from doing something, and following this the aim of translation would be to get the effect of deterrence across effectively without dwelling in the nitty-gritty of the linguistics.

Things are not always so clear-cut, of course. We have mentioned that all texts are hybrid in some way, and therefore it is completely possible for different parts of a single text to be translated in different ways. Consider a recipe book by celebrity British chef Jamie Oliver. If we see a recipe book as a kind of instruction manual, then it is both informative and operative: it provides information (the ingredients and their quantities) at the same time as it prompts readers to take a designated course of action ('heat in the oven for 20 mins'; 'do not add in the basil leaves at this point'). According to Reiss's theory, that would mean writing style is a secondary consideration in translating recipes.

In the case of Jamie Oliver, however, the chef/writer is known for his candid personality, and this comes through partly in his quirky and irreverent use of English. A translator of Oliver's recipe book thus needs to take into account this anomalous aspect of the language; otherwise a different persona of the chef could emerge in the TT. Tanner (2013), for example, observes that the German translation of Oliver's book 'bowdlerises' some strongly colloquial expressions, thereby turning his discursive persona from an 'expert friend' to an 'authoritative teacher'.

Try this

Let us look at a recipe by Jamie Oliver, available on his website. Here is one for his 'Breakfast Doughnuts': www.jamieoliver.com/recipes/breakfast-recipes/breakfast-doughnuts/?family-food-category=105052.
Read the method for preparation, and pay special attention to the imperative verbs. There is almost a sense of humour in the way some of these verbs are used. To make Breakfast Doughnuts we are supposed to '*Tear* the stones out of the dates', '*Blitz* [in a food processor] until combined', and '*Jiggle* and shake the pan'. (In another recipe we are asked to 'swirl a splash' of water and 'whack' some lemongrass sticks!) How might you render these verbs in another language, such that the TL reader does not only get the culinary instructions, but also the jovial, light-hearted character of the piece as a whole? Try translating a few of these imperative sentences into a language of your choice, and see if you are able to translate Jamie Oliver's down-to-earth, 'expert friend' persona.

Corollary to this is Christiane Nord's idea of **documentary** versus **instrumental** translation (Nord 2014: 47). The first of the pair refers to a translation process that replays a communicative event that has transpired between the ST author and the ST audience. Here there is no intention to conceal the identity of the translation as such: the TT reader is made aware that what s/he is reading has originally appeared elsewhere in some other language. This information could, for example, be flagged out in the form of the author's and translator's names on the cover page of a translated book (the usual structure being 'Translated from the [SL] by [name of translator]').

And because the status of the translation qua translation and the identity of the author are usually explicated, the translator is obliged to adhere to the ST closely, even to the point of producing an **exoticising translation** (Nord 2014: 48). This mode of translation is used when it is important for the reader to know who said what, how, and to whom in the original context, as for example a presidential candidate speaking to his/her supporters. Expressive texts normally require documentary treatment in translation, with fictional translation being the most common.

Exoticising translation

A method of translation that works through the discrete textual units of the ST closely. This kind of translation produces a 'foreign' flavour in the TT by way of its 'translationese' style, and normally requires more cognitive effort on the part of the TT reader. It is the diametrical opposite of a more naturalised translation, which tends toward absorbing the linguistic and cultural peculiarities of the ST into the TL to provide for a fluent, effortless read.

This calls to mind Lawrence Venuti's (2008) influential notion of **domestication** versus **foreignisation**. Although Venuti's concepts do not strictly belong under the rubric of applied translation studies (his agenda being more ideological-political in nature), it has its roots in an early theory of practice: Friedrich Schleiermacher's (2012 [1813]) idea that in translating, we have one of two options: (1) bring the foreign text toward the reader (refashioned by Venuti as domestication); (2) bring the reader toward the foreign text (Venuti's foreignisation). Venuti celebrates the latter approach and applies it rigorously in his translation of non-Anglophone literature into English. Once again we witness how a conceptual translation theory, critiquing unequal power relations between languages in this case, has ramifications for applied practice.

Other examples include: interlinear translation (e.g., glossing a foreign language utterance morpheme-by-morpheme in linguistics textbooks); literal translation (e.g., when dealing with direct quotes in news articles); and philological translation (e.g., translation of Greek and Latin classics at the level of syntax) (48).

 Instrumental translation, on the other hand, refers to a translation process that intends to perform a new communicative event in the target context. Although based on some original text, the translation often camouflages its real identity and acts as if it were written in the TL. It is immaterial whether or not the TT reader is aware of the fact that s/he is reading a translation: the TT does not *represent* the ST but *stands in* for the ST. In other words, the TT functionally substitutes the ST in the TL culture, which makes it unnecessary to explicate the identity of the ST and SL author.

Instrumental translation applies when the TT is supposed to function as an autonomous entity in the target context, the implication being that it should not sound too exotic, as that would expose its foreign provenance and possibly compromise its efficacy in the target culture. This means that the translator need not be subservient to the ST and has more space for textual manoeuvre; in some cases the translator can rewrite the ST if doing so allows the translation to serve its purpose.

The translation of operative texts would fall under this category. Would you be interested to know, for instance, that the SKII advertisement in your local shopping centre is in fact derived from some original copy in another part of the planet? To a potential consumer, this information would be most irrelevant as regards his or her desire to purchase the product. The translated copy could well be different from the original copy (assuming there is one), but that is perfectly acceptable because it is intended to replace the original in another market with a different language background. Other examples from Nord include translating operating instructions, adapting a novel for children, and self-translating one's own writing (Nord 2014: 51).

Function is not always an inherent property of the text; there is no simple one-to-one correspondence between text type and translation strategy. A play, for example, can be treated as an expressive text following Reiss's typology, and therefore translated with close attention to its formal structures – Nord's documentary translation. Imagine, however, that the same play is appropriated to advance some cause that lies beyond the scope of literature as such – perhaps to educate the public on a social issue or to promote a political agenda. This would turn the play into an operative text that aims to motivate the receiver to take a particular course of action. The ST may accordingly be subject to all kinds of manipulation in translation, which is instrumental translation in Nord's terms. A single text may therefore be translated differently according to different contingent needs, and this falls outside the purview of text-type theory.

Translatorial action

Functionalists have taken translation not just beyond the text itself but also beyond text-type and into the real world. This is best encapsulated by the phrase *translatorisches Handeln*, rendered in English as 'translatorial action' or 'translational action'. This is the title of a 1984 book by Justa Holz-Mänttäri, who treats translation as one among many possible forms of intercultural transfer, 'a complex action designed to achieve a particular purpose' (cited in Nord 2014: 13). This is a highly significant definition. By conceiving of translation as designed action, it affords a kinetic and proactive dimension to translation, thereby giving the translator a brand-new image. Whereas hitherto the translator is positioned in respect to and in service of either the ST author or the TL reader (or both), in the model of translatorial action, the translator assumes much greater agency: s/he is now an expert possessing the prerequisite skills and knowledge to perform an intercultural task.

This contrasts sharply with the conventional and still persistent image of a translator as a word worker operating not just in servitude but also in isolation. For Holz-Mänttäri, the translator actively contributes to a chain of semiotic events (i.e., communicative acts involving language as well as non-linguistic means of producing meaning) that constitute intercultural communication; hence translatorial action is more precisely defined as 'the process of producing a message transmitter of a certain kind, designed to be employed in superordinate action systems in order to coordinate actional and communicative cooperation' (cited in Nord 2014: 13).

This formulation sounds a little abstruse and technical, so let us paraphrase it into a more digestible form:

Translatorial action
Translation is a process of delivering a text or some other mode of intercultural mediation, embedded within a larger communicative event to actively facilitate cooperation between parties situated in different languages and cultures.

The idea of translatorial action serves to move us away from the microtextual idea of translation as a simplistic transference of language material from source to target that is executed in vacuo, that is, without interaction with other related processes. It also reconceptualises the product of translation as an *artefact* (which can of course still be a text in the traditional sense) that is fully operative, thus enabling us to release our understanding of translating from linguistics-based and text-based models.

The new model requires us instead to think in terms of how translation actually works, not on the basis of constructing linear correspondences between source and target texts but as a *holistic entity* engaged in action. The term 'message transmitter' (*Botschaftsträger*) suggests that translation is a functional instrument that supports the movement of information across languages, exceeding the mere process of language transfer. A translation is 'designed to be employed', which means its production requires technical and creative expertise, and brings along its own logistics; and as with all commercial output it is produced with a particular cause in mind. What is this cause? It is 'to coordinate actional and communicative cooperation', for translatorial actions are not discrete operations, but rather integral processes that feed into 'superordinate action systems'; in other words, they are one of several stages within a larger workflow.

Following the model of translatorial action, translation takes on an interactional and interpersonal dimension, where a translator acts as a mediating figure in situations 'where differences in verbal and non-verbal behaviour, expectations, knowledge and perspectives are such that there is not enough common ground for the sender and receiver to communicate effectively by themselves' (Nord 2014: 17). Interestingly, in these kinds of situation, the translator's intervention may or may not involve translating. Nord (2014: 15, 17) provides the following example: a businessman approaches an English translator to have a letter, drafted in Spanish, to be translated into English for a small firm in a certain country. The translator, whose has lived in the latter country for several years, is aware that English may not be the working language for small firms there, and Chinese may be a better medium. She thus advises the prospective client to have his letter translated into Chinese instead, and recommends another translator she knows. In this case, the English translator does not expressly perform an interlingual task; rather, she is acting as an intercultural advisor or consultant by tapping into her knowledge of the target culture in question. By virtue of that we say she is performing a translatorial action, which 'may involve giving advice and perhaps even *warning against* communicating in the intended way' (17), as the example above shows.

A translatorial action can encompass translation, but it often moves beyond **translation proper** – that is, the mere transfer of meaning from one language to another. In other words, translation 'is seen as *the particular variety of translational action* which is based on a source text' (Vermeer 2012 [1989]: 191; emphasis added); it exists alongside other varieties, which are not necessarily grounded in some ST, for example,

---

Translation proper

Also called **interlingual translation,** this is the most ordinary sense of trans-lating, involving the transfer of meaning from one language into a different language. By contrast, **intralingual translation** refers to the transfer of mean-ing *within* a language, for example, paraphrasing (rewording the meaning of a text using the same language) or translating between different varieties/ registers of the same language. Yet another type of translation is **intersemi-otic translation,** where a verbal text is rendered into a nonverbal form, or vice versa. The adaptation of the Harry Potter series into Hollywood film is a prime example of this latter kind of translation. This interlingual-intralingual-interse-miotic typology was first proposed by the renowned linguist Roman Jakobson in his article 'On Linguistic Aspects of Translation' (Jakobson 2012 [1959]) and is widely influential in translation studies.

---

a marketing consultant's review of the cultural situation in another country. Nord (2014: 17) considers another hypothetical example where a technical translator is asked to translate into German an English oper-ating manual for a machine. The problem is that the English manual is full of errors; translating it as it is would create a problematic TT, which could potentially cause risk to people who operate the machine based on the translated instructions. To create a usable translation, the trans-lator in question consults an engineer on how the machine works and then writes a German copy based on the acquired knowledge. Here the translator is performing an interlingual task, but does not rely on the ST; instead s/he writes a new TT that deals with the same subject mat-ter. This rewriting is justified by the purpose of the task at hand: to pro-duce a translation that guides TT users to properly and safely operate the machine.

We mentioned that a translatorial action dovetails into a larger frame of intercultural communication. For example, in the chain of production and circulation of commodities or social services, manufacturing, mar-keting, sales, and consumption constitute the major fields. Translation affiliates itself to the marketing component, with a view to adding value to sales (Ho 2004: 222–223). Translatorial action therefore entails sev-eral actors, of which the translator is one. These various actors and their respective roles are summarised in Table 3.1.

Table 3.1 Actors involved in translatorial action

Actor	Role	Example/Remarks
Initiator/ Commissioner	Starts off the translation process; defines purpose of translation. The Initiator is the individual or institution who needs the translation, whereas the Commissioner is the individual or institution who manages the translation project.	Suppose, under local regulations, a public company needs to make its financial documents (e.g., announcements, circulars, annual reports) available in two official languages. When it hires a translation agency to manage the translation project, it becomes the Initiator; the agency may in turn delegate the task to freelance translators, in which case it serves as Commissioner. Sometimes, the Initiator of the translation doubles up as the Commissioner, in which case there is no distinction between the two.
Source-Text Producer	The actual person crafting the text to be translated and responsible for all linguistic and stylistic choices in the ST. Theoretically this is distinct from the Sender – the individual or institution *deploying* a text to communicate with target readers.	The public company above may choose to hire an agency to write the original financial documents in the first place; this hired agency can then be seen as the Source-Text Producer. Where the Source-Text Producer is the Initiator (or Sender), the distinction becomes irrelevant.
Translator	An expert in translatorial action; executes translation work based on requirements in the *commission* (or *brief*). The *commission* is a document that contains details of the project, including the translator's fees, dateline of submission, how and where the document will be used, by whom and for who, formatting requirements, etc.	The final product of the translatorial action may be a piece of translation; it can also be a summary or adaptation of the source text, depending on the purpose of the task. In some cases, the translator may even advise the Commissioner that translation would not serve his/her intended purpose and hence should not be executed. For instance, a translator might advise that the tagline of an annual report issued by the public company can be used as it is without translation.

(Continued)

73

Table 3.1 Actors involved in translatorial action (*Continued*)

Actor	Role	Example/Remarks
Target-Text User	The individual or institution putting the translation to use for a specific purpose.	The public company will use the translation as an informative-legal document to provide information to its existing and potential shareholders. Oftentimes the Target-Text User is the Initiator who triggers the translation project in the first place.
Target-Text Receiver	The individual or institution consuming the translation. Theoretically a distinction is possible between Addressee (the projected reader of the TT seen from the perspective of the Source-Text Producer) and the Target-Text Receiver (the actual person or group consuming the TT).	The Target-Text Receiver is the end-user of the translation, e.g., the reader of the translated financial documents issued by the public company; this reader may rely on the information contained in the translated documents to take certain courses of action, e.g., to purchase shares in the public company.

Note: Based on Nord (2014: 19–22); the example and remarks are mine.

Translatorial action in crosscultural publishing: An example

In many situations, a single individual or institution may assume more than one role. For the purpose of illustration, let us look at a case of cross-cultural publishing, which involves and goes beyond the full spectrum of roles described in Table 3.1. Cambridge University Press (CUP) has published a large volume of English books under the series 'Introduction to Chinese Culture'. Some of these titles include: *Chinese Ceramics*; *Ancient Chinese Inventions*; *Chinese Bronze Ware*; *Peking Opera*; *Traditional Chinese Medicine*; *Chinese Myths and Legends*; *Chinese Vernacular Dwellings*; *Chinese Kung Fu*, to name just a few.

These are translations from books originally written in Chinese, but even before the CUP volumes came about, the books already had their English versions. Both the writing of the original books and their initial English translations were commissioned and published by China Intercontinental Press (CIP) under the auspices of the China Book International (CBI) programme, a state-funded initiative that aims to disseminate Chinese culture worldwide through translation. The initial English translations, all done by Chinese translators, were subsequently republished by CUP with stylistic amendments. Notably, the earlier translations were fine-tuned to render them more idiomatic in English. Whereas the substantive content remained the same, its framing was changed (for example, some chapters in the original CIP translation were collapsed in the revised CUP version), along with adjustments in illustration and layout.

In this case, we say that CBI is the Initiator, as it starts off the entire project by funding it. The Commissioner is obviously the Chinese publisher CIP. We have a Source-Text Producer, that is, the authors of the Chinese texts on which the translation is based, as well as a Translator on the Chinese side.

But things get more complicated from this point, because the translation travels from China to the UK through special copyright arrangements between the two publishers. CUP would have its own editorial team to modify the translation, illustration, and layout; thus CUP serves as Commissioner for the text's new English edition, and whoever revises the translation functions as Translator/Editor. The Target-Text User and Target-Text Receiver are also differentiated: on China's side, the User would be CBI, which uses the translated texts for the purpose of spreading knowledge about Chinese culture.

The Receiver is a little tricky to identify: it can be assumed that native Chinese persons would normally not voluntarily choose to read a Chinese book in English translation, except perhaps for the purpose of learning English as a foreign language. The Receivers in this case could be expatriates working and living in China, as well as ethnic Chinese communities outside of mainland China, such as Hong Kong and Singapore, where English is an official language. On the UK side, the User of CUP's books could be institutions that deliver introductory courses on Chinese culture to a Western audience (e.g., Confucius Institute), and the Receiver would be the teachers and students of those courses as well as other non-Chinese readers who might be interested in Chinese culture.

This example shows how translating is imbricated in the complex network of international publishing. By assigning roles to the multiple agents involved in the process of writing, translating, editing, and publishing, and by highlighting the chain-like nature of the workflow, we can begin to appreciate translation as participating within a broader discursive process. The production of a series of Chinese books, already translated into English, in revised English versions by a UK university press is a complex crosscultural event; it involves translation proper but also far more than that – copyright transfer, revision of translation, reformatting, installing new visuals, and so forth. That is the essence of translatorial action, which is an agentive mode of communication across languages and cultures that includes and goes beyond mere translating.

Skopos theory

Closely aligned with the concept of translatorial action is skopos theory (*Skopostheorie*), championed by Hans Vermeer in his article 'Skopos and Commission in Translational Action' (Vermeer 2012 [1989]). *Skopos* is a Greek word meaning 'purpose'. The theory states that 'one does not translate a source text in a void, as it were, but always according to a given skopos or commission' (202). This is conceived as a general theory with several entailments, stipulated as 'rules' by Reiss and Vermeer in their book *Towards a General Theory of Translational Action*. (Note that in addition to *skopos*, other idiosyncratic terms are used, such as *translatum*, which simply refers to the product of translation, namely, the TT. We do not need to concern ourselves too much with these terms.)

General rules of skopos theory

1. A *translatum* is determined by its *skopos*.
2. A *translatum* is an offer of information in a target culture and language about an offer of information in a source culture and language.
3. A *translatum* is a unique, irreversible mapping of a source-culture offer of information.
4. A *translatum* must be coherent in itself.
5. A *translatum* must be coherent with the source text.
6. These rules are interdependent and linked hierarchically in the order set out above.

(Reiss & Vermeer 2014 [1984]: 107)

These rules are arranged in order of importance (Rule 6), with skopos (Rule 1) as the overarching principle. The expression 'offer of information' (Rule 2) rearticulates the function of translation as providing an informational service, as opposed to simply reproducing a given source text. Depending on the purpose of the commission, a translation can turn out to be a different creature than its original, though this is not always necessarily the case. This means that if we back-translate the TT into the SL, we may or may not obtain something that resembles the ST (Rule 3, the rule of irreversibility); in other words, the back-translation test cannot be used as a test of accuracy in this case – indeed 'accuracy' becomes a problematic notion in respect of skopos theory. To fully serve its function, the TT must cohere itself to the receiving context of TL readers (Rule 4). This '(internal) coherence rule' overrides the so-called 'fidelity rule' (Rule 5), which states that the TT must correspond to the ST in terms of the latter's offer of information. Apparently, then, fidelity to the original text is of a low priority in skopos theory; but as we shall see shortly, this does not give us the licence to wilfully ignore the original text under all circumstances.

Skopos theory basically sees translation as a goal-oriented action, which in turn may be embedded within a higher-level action, in a recursive scaling at different orders. We might see translatorial action as a superordinate concept, with skopos theory catering specifically to textual translation. In this sense, skopos theory is an offshoot of translatorial action, contributing to the event of cross- or intercultural communication. Vermeer describes this relation as follows: 'Translational action leads to a "target text" (not necessarily a verbal one); translation leads to a *translatum* (i.e. the resulting translated text), as a particular variety of target text' (Vermeer 2012 [1989]: 191).

Under skopos theory, the raison d'être of translation is to serve a purpose that is determined on a contingent basis; it thus follows that the criteria with which one assesses the quality of a translation cannot be based on purely linguistic concerns, but rather on whether a translation fulfils its stipulated purpose. To put this in a rather extreme way: if the translation of, say, an advertisement for a cosmetic product aims at increasing the sales of that product, then the translation is deemed to have passed the mark if it is indeed proven that it has contributed positively to sales. Whether the original advertising copy is translated closely or radically rewritten (or is positioned somewhere in the middle) is quite beside the point as far as hardcore functionalists are concerned.

The skopos of a translation commission need not always be commercially driven: a scholar may decide to translate a collection of poems in such a way that would make it well-received in academia. This skopos would motivate him to insert lengthy footnotes and learned commentaries. Once again, from a functionalist perspective, this translator's use of paratexts (i.e., textual material outside of and in supplement to the body text) is not in itself right or wrong. It is rather the final outcome, that is, the reception (favourable, lukewarm, unfavourable) of the translated poems by the target users, in this case literary critics and university faculty, that determines the efficacy of the translation. If, however, the translator's skopos is to popularise the poems, to avail them to a general public or a novice readership, then he would probably decide to do away with those footnotes, which would make the ordinary reader head straight for the exit.

Who, then, decides the skopos, and how is this communicated to the translator? This is where we need a 'commission' (*Auftrag*), defined as: 'the instruction, given by oneself or by someone else, to carry out a given action – here: to translate' (Vermeer 2012 [1989]: 199). A commission explicates the *goal* of the translation assignment and the *conditions* under which the assignment is undertaken, including such practical matters as payment and dateline (199).

Importantly, Vermeer opens up the possibility for the translator to negotiate with the client on these issues, 'for the client may occasionally have an imprecise or even false picture of the way a text might be received in the target culture. Here the translator should be able to make argumentative suggestions' (199). This last statement is critical: in line with Holz-Mänttäri's idea of translatorial action, it affirms the professional status of the translator, giving him/her the right and responsibility of a consultant who may advise the client or commissioner on the nature and complexity of the task. This affords the translator the identity of a trained expert who is not obliged to unconditionally abide by the ST; s/he is not merely a language operator, but one who is fully engaged in translatorial action, involving textual translation alongside other modes of action that can lubricate communication across languages and cultures.

Skopos theory is sometimes criticised as going too far in 'dethroning' (Vermeer's term), or subverting the binding importance of, the ST: recall that the 'fidelity rule' (Rule 5) that connects the TT to the ST is least important in this theory. There seems to be the perceived danger that the translator can do anything s/he wants with the ST since any manipulation can theoretically be justified by invoking 'purpose' as a line of defence.

But the ST's dethronement is not the ultimate aim of skopos theory. The ST can potentially be dethroned if the purpose of the translatorial action requires this to happen; but there is nothing inevitable about this situation. Vermeer maintains that 'True translation, with an adequate skopos, does not mean that the translator *must* adapt to the customs and usage of the target culture, only that he *can* so adapt' (Vermeer 2012 [1989]: 198). In literary translation, for example, the governing skopos would be 'maximally faithful imitation of the original' (198), Vermeer so advocates. (We must add, though, that this is just the predominant type of skopos in literary translation, especially where poetry is concerned. In some circumstances it might be possible for a translator to provide a relatively free rendition to give an equivalent of the aesthetic sensation of the original, given that there is consensus among the poet, the translator, and the publisher on this latter skopos.) We can see Reiss's text-type theory coming into the picture here (she is after all Vermeer's co-researcher), for the skopos of translation is in part determined by the type of text in question.

Hence, contrary to the belief that skopos theory encourages the translator to take audacious liberties with the ST,

the theory equally well accommodates the opposite type of translation, deliberately marked, with the intention of expressing source-culture features by target-culture means. Everything between these two extremes is likewise possible, including hybrid cases. To know what the point of a translation is, to be conscious of the action – that is the goal of the skopos theory. (Vermeer 2012 [1989]: 201)

In this connection, Christiane Nord offers a theoretical corrective to bring the ST back into the picture. She proposes that functionality must be complemented with 'loyalty', an interpersonal concept that 'commits the translator bilaterally to the source and the target sides' (Nord 2014: 125). The translator exhibits loyalty to the source side by ensuring that the translation does not depart from the source author's intention; the latter is supposed to act as a restraint on the translator's scope of textual treatment, to prevent him or her from 'imposing [his/her] culture-specific concept on members of another culture community' (125). Nord gives the example of a Spanish book in which the author sympathises with the Castro regime in Cuba; the German translator, however, moderates this viewpoint, making the tone of the book more objective. This breaches the loyalty component even though it may have fulfilled the publisher's skopos. Nord opines that the translator 'should have argued this point with the initiator or perhaps have refused to produce the translation on ethical grounds' (127).

Translation as language solution

Given its strong end-user orientation, skopos theory proves to be the most relevant theoretical model as far as the translation and interpreting (T&I) industry is concerned. A case in point is Capita Translation and Interpreting, a leading **language solutions** provider in the UK with an international clientele under its belt. The term 'language solutions' denotes a wide range of language-related services including but not limited to translation. At its core it constitutes a business model that aims to tailor-make a communications package – this could be a simple document or a complex webpage design project – to serve the needs of the client. The idea of language solutions is therefore a fluid and contingent one, and the pertinent approach to translation is one that is fully in accord with skopos theory.

Figure 3.1 shows Capita's model of translation. Notice the mission statement on the left of the diagram, which reads: 'This [the type of translation service] can vary from project to project depending on what you need at the time. By gathering the key information, we then use our expertise to ensure the correct solution is deployed by us, to meet those objectives in the delivery.' This statement exemplifies the principal themes of translatorial action (translation as an expertise that includes

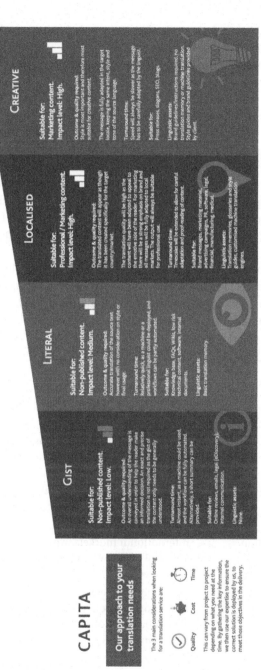

Figure 3.1 Gradations of translation in the T&I industry

information gathering) and skopos theory (translation as a solution delivered to meet stipulated objectives).

The core part of Figure 3.1 encapsulates how Capita conceptualises their services as a gradation of different levels, ranging from **Gist** translation, to **Literal** translation, through **Localised** translation (more on this below), and terminating at **Creative** translation (cf. Newmark's model in Figure 2.1). Read Figure 3.1 carefully, and you will find that each level constitutes a different type of language solution, caters to different purposes, entails different resources (glossaries, translation technologies, etc.), and requires varying lengths of time to complete. The diagram embodies the spirit of skopos, namely, that there is no such thing as a single correct translation to a ST, a one-size-fits-all solution that works in every situation; each translation task must be treated on a case-by-case basis and yield its own specific solution.

Under the rubric of language solutions, what specific services are available in the T&I industry and what is the role of translation in each of them? Table 3.2 shows a sampling of these services, adapted from Capita's website.

Table 3.2 Types of service in the T&I industry

Service	Nature
Translation	Renders written communications from one language into another using human translators
Interpreting	Renders spoken communications from one language into another using human interpreters, either via telephone or in a face-to-face environment
Audiovisual translation (AVT)	Includes multilingual subtitling, voice-over, and dubbing services
Digital content and website localisation	Reconfigures websites to cater to multiple international markets, which is increasingly essential as the world becomes more and more connected
e-Learning and training translation	Translates courseware with the help of technological tools such as **translation memory** (TM: a digital tool that allows users to create term banks to store, manage, and extract complex terminology)

Software localisation	Adapts the language and functionality of software products to the specifics of a target market
Design and typesetting	Value-adds to conventional translation with desktop publishing services, such as formatting and layout. This ensures that the translated text (presentation slides, annual reports, user manuals or marketing collateral, etc.) looks as good as the source file and prevents issues like overflowing text and incorrect line-wrapping
Transcreation and copywriting	Develops or adapts new content instead of just 'straight' translation; this includes copywriting, image selection, font changes, and other transformations that tailor the message to ensure relevance for target global audiences
Transcription	Creates written transcriptions for a range of different content types, which may or may not involve two languages

Adapted from: www.capitatranslationinterpreting.com/language-services/.

The range of services listed in Table 3.2 should convince us that in the T&I industry, translation is not just about moving words across pages; it is subsumed under a host of language solutions, wherein translation partakes as a process that facilitates the flow of texts, ideas, and commodities across languages and cultures. In this context, not only does the notion of translation extend beyond verbal language (e.g., in audiovisual translation and software localisation), it also puts translation into a mixed bag of services. Apart from the first three categories (translation, interpreting, audiovisual translation), the other services listed in Table 3.2 involve processes other than translating (e.g., typesetting, transcription, transcreation) but in which more than one language can be involved. We also see the use of technologies (e.g., translation memory) beyond the mere word processor or online dictionary. This is the condition of translation practice in the industry: it is purpose-oriented, commercially driven, and embedded within a network of linguistic as well as non-linguistic processes. This functionalist model of translation is a very different creature than that espoused in the equivalence paradigm.

Further real-life applications

It is merely for convenience that we have treated text-type theory, translatorial action, and skopos theory separately; in praxis, they are always considered in integrated fashion. We have seen, for example, that the purpose of a translation is related to the functional type of the text to be translated. A singular type of text can also be put to differential uses (hence yielding different translational treatments) depending on the communicative event in which it is embedded. The following paragraphs will bring together the theoretical strands we have discussed by illustrating how they operate in tandem in actual translation practice, based on anecdotal accounts by practitioners.

Translaboration (translation + collaboration)

The interactional-interpersonal feature of translatorial action requires the translator-as-actor to keep a close eye on different processes within an intercultural communicative event. To illustrate this, let us look at a case of making multilingual questionnaires, as reported by the German translator Ilse Freiburg. A questionnaire is deceptively easy to translate. On the face of it, it looks like an informative text, and based on Reiss's theory we should go straight for the content and ignore the wording. But remember that the purpose of using a questionnaire is to elicit responses so as to identify tendencies on certain phenomena. And so we need to make sure that the questions asked in different languages are indeed the same questions, that is, respondents reading a question in different languages must understand it in exactly the same way, otherwise the whole purpose would be defeated. There are invisible pitfalls such as the comparability and consistency of the same survey in different languages. Freiburg (2015: 11) tells us that '[t]he prerequisites for a successful cross-cultural survey are well-designed questionnaires and stop-quality translations that ensure comparability. To prevent inconsistencies, it is vital that the coordinator, client and translator work closely together and learn from each other.'

Though Freiburg is a translator by profession, in actual assignments she often serves as a project manager and coordinates with consultants representing a client; this demonstrates our earlier point that in translatorial action, a translator's job scope often spills over into other aspects: 'As the coordinator, it is important that I fully understand *what the customer wants to measure* with each item/question, so that I can support my colleagues in the subsequent cross-national translation process' (Freiburg 2015: 12; emphasis added). This statement shows the centrality of the client's intentions in respect of the translation commission, and highlights how Freiburg mediates between the client and her translator colleagues. Based on her understanding of the client's purpose, Freiburg then proceeds to compile explanatory notes and relevant contextual information (e.g., information about the company in question and its products, etc.). Such ancillary information provides resources that can be useful when a survey question is ambiguous or complex. Research of this kind is essential to translatorial action, even though it does not belong to the domain of translation proper.

There are linguistic issues to deal with, of course, such as the presence of locale-specific words that find no equivalents in other countries or cultures, in which case generic terms are used. Freiburg (2015: 12) gives the example of *Räumliche Gegebenheiten*, translated as 'available space' even though the German phrase is a more general term for lighting, noise, ambient conditions, and space. An even more telling case is how the translator may sometimes intervene by modifying a ST while keeping to its overall semantic and pragmatic meaning. The example here is *Meine Arbeit macht mir Spaß*, literally 'My work is fun'. Freiburg determines that the German clause, if more properly formulated, should be *Meine Arbeit macht mir Freude,* and thus proposes that 'I enjoy my work' would better reflect the intention of the original question, even though that is not a literal translation of the original German. Clearly in this case the translator is not a word worker subservient to the ST but an intercultural consultant who uses her professional knowledge to actively mediate between languages. As an agent (not servant) she intervenes where necessary, and this may involve adjusting the ST formulation in the translation.

Other considerations include the locale where the translated questionnaire will be used. For example, the same concept may have different lexical realisations in different varieties of a language, as in the German *Pausenraum* ('rest area') versus *Jausenstation* as used in Austria. In the case of Portuguese and Spanish, Freiburg (2015: 13) states that European versions of these languages have to be passed on to native speakers of Brazilian Portuguese and Latin American Spanish for adaptation, due to the considerable differences between Continental and Latin American varieties. This attests to the functionalist criterion of prioritising the linguistic habits of the Target-Text User and Receiver. Cooperation among translators as well as with other stakeholders is the key here, as it is in the area of quality assessment: 'Ideally, we discuss our work with another translator who is familiar with translating questionnaires. Adjudication is made jointly by the national affiliates on the customer's site and with the translators' (13). This foregrounds the collaborative nature of translatorial action, also known as **translaboration** (Alfer 2015).

Freiburg reveals how she and her team had to work closely with their customers in the iterative process of revising and fine-tuning the terminology used in multilingual questionnaires. Importantly, she reports how she needs to 'convince our customers of the added value they get from professionally translated questionnaires' (2015: 13) when negotiating translation fees. Practical considerations such as these, which are irrelevant to the equivalence paradigm, are pertinent to the model of translatorial action. Here the translator provides a professional service for a (hopefully reasonable) fee, seeks to add value to the entire chain of production and circulation of a product or service, and, to this end, works in coordination with other parties and processes in the chain.

On clients and end-users

The idea of skopos brings our attention to the purpose of translating a text; and because this purpose is dictated to a large extent by the client (if there is one), the theory places a heavy weightage on the client's expectation. In the case where the client is not the end-user, the latter's circumstance would need to be factored in as well. From a contrastive-linguistic (i.e., non-functionalist) perspective, the translator's challenge is to tackle differences that are inherent within the structures of the SL and the TL; the translatability of a text is ingrained in the abstract space between two languages.

The lesson that functionalist theories teach us is, however, very different, namely, the nitty-gritty of translation is governed in large part by how the TT is put into use *in an actual situation*, as well as the crosscultural issues that TL users might face. There is nothing abstract in this, and translatability is not determined a priori as a potentiality, that is to say, before a piece of text is being tossed into the real world. Translatability becomes an issue by virtue of the fact that a text is translated to be used by someone for a particular reason.

Applying skopos theory to translation means to manoeuvre linguistic resources while bearing the client or end-user in mind. Take the example of the 'recitals' of a legal agreement where the contractual parties are named. Here different conventions exist for different languages, so the question is how to negotiate between them. The translator Gwen Clayton considers how the Japanese use *kou, otsu*, and *hei* (literally, A, B, and C; or First, Second, and Third [parties]) to name the parties to an agreement, and diagnoses that 'if you use only these terms, or even the initials of each company's name, it may be hard to be consistent and the person reading the document will not know who is being referred to without constantly turning back to the first page' (Clayton 2015: 16).

Based on this diagnosis, Clayton decides that she would name either the companies or their roles in the agreement (Buyer, Seller, etc.), a practice that is also in line with English conventions for the genre. Note that this is not just a linguistic consideration: from Clayton's account we see that her foremost priority is not whether the specific lexical items are correctly conveyed in and of themselves, but whether the reader of the translated contract will be clear (or confused) as to which party is being referred to. The final linguistic intervention (e.g., translating Party A as 'Buyer', Party B as 'Seller') may seem trivial, but the decision-making process demonstrates the translator's role as a service provider who not merely tackles interlingual issues but ensures that the translation can properly serve the needs of the client and end-user. As Clayton reminds us, it is important for translators to read 'with an eye to the broader purpose of the document' (Clayton 2015: 17) rather than focus solely on the words themselves.

Clayton further shares with us that the register of the TT can be influenced by client expectations, which suggests that functionalist factors can override linguistic ones. For example, when faced with a text written in an archaic register in Japanese, should it be translated into plain English, or should it be sprinkled with Latin terms 'to recreate the more edifying effect of the Meiji period phrasing?' Clayton's advice is simple: 'try to find out in advance' (Clayton 2015: 17). Find out from who? The client, of course. While it makes more linguistic sense to replicate the register of the Japanese original by using an ornate style in English, some clients may prefer a TT that reads with ease. Under the functionalist paradigm, the client's wishes shall prevail.

In commercial settings profit motives may offset or cancel linguistic concerns; this again underlines our main point about skopos: that translational decisions may be made less on the basis of language per se but on the interests of the commissioner or client. Patent translation is a case in point. The translator Michelle Deeter relates her experience, from which she concludes that the translator's lexical choice in dealing with patent applications is conditioned by a product's patentability, utility, and novelty. In one assignment Deeter (2015) encountered a Chinese text that mentioned riding a vehicle called *diandong zhuli che*, literally 'electrical assisted-power car'; she translated this as 'electric bicycle' because the fact that the vehicle was 'ridden' (a verb that must have occurred somewhere in the same document) means it could not be a car. Deeter's English version was, however, amended by a more senior translator to 'electrically-assisted vehicle'. Linguistically speaking, the revised translation is less concise and also less precise. So why this revision, considering that we ordinarily value concision and precision in all forms of writing?

As it turned out, the senior translator amended Deeter's version not on the basis of linguistic grounds; the new translation afforded a broader and more ambiguous interpretation, and broadness and ambiguity happen to be a plus-point as far as patent applications are concerned. Deeter's example shows us that the translator can be constrained by the purpose of the assignment in question – in this case to facilitate the successful bid for a patent. This purpose governs the contingent strategy adopted by the patent translator – 'each word needs to be specific enough to prove that it is a new idea, yet broad enough to include multiple possibilities' (14). Although Deeter's linguistic interpretation was correct, her translation was deemed not to serve the ultimate goal of the patent job perfectly. The phrase 'electrically-assisted vehicle' provides for a much wider scope than 'electric bicycle' while still falling within the domain of automobiles, thus fulfilling the particular skopos of this commission.

Research as a component of translatorial action

A conventional conception of translation is to see it as a linear process of verbal transfer at the level of language, with the erroneous assumption that there is a substantive core of meaning encapsulated within a particular stretch of text. Accordingly, the translator's horizon could be kept safely within the discursive perimeters of the text s/he is translating.

This would be the case if one were translating all the time within the protective walls of the foreign language classroom. In real life, however, the translator often has to undertake supplementary tasks that fall beyond the text and even beyond language as such. This is because the knowledge fields of ST readers and TT readers can be very different, such that an unmediated SL-to-TL transfer could lead to a shortfall in terms of what is communicated.

Note that this is different from **explicitation**, introduced in Chapter 2. Explicitation in translation means making explicit what remains implicit in the ST, normally at the level of the language (e.g., explicating the gender when translating from a SL that does not lexically encode gender categories). This type of intervention typically does not exceed 'using explicatory words or phrases, employing cohesive devices, clearing up grammatical ambiguities, and so on' (Munday 2009: 187), and relies on the translator's intuitive competence of the SL and TL. On the other hand, the type of intervention we are dealing with at the functionalist level goes beyond the mere 'tweaking' of the ST at the level of lexis, grammar, or even discourse, and entails additional research. Real-world translation is client-based and user-based, not language-based. This means the translator must sometimes double up as a researcher and/or consultant to gather more information as might be necessary for the intercultural task at hand.

Some examples are in order. One key challenge in translating history texts, as Allison Brown tells us, 'is that of understanding historical concepts and terminology, and rendering them appropriately in the vocabulary of the discourse familiar to English-speaking historians' (Brown 2015: 13). This is especially pertinent when the translator is not a historian by training, whence research must become an integral part of the translating process. Translating history texts additionally requires 'an understanding of different sensibilities and knowledge of history for different audiences' (13). Because ST and TT audiences may have different historical backgrounds, the translator may need to supply background information that may have been taken for granted by the ST author. In Brown's case, she was further requested by the publisher to insert footnotes in the translation to clarify certain points left unclear in the ST, and that necessitated research into the relevant subject matter (15).

In addressing historically sensitive topics such as the Nazi regime, for example, a knowledgeable translator should know that German authors tend to distance themselves from Nazi discourse by placing words such as 'Aryan' and 'Third Reich' in quotation marks, whereas English texts tend to leave them as they are. Euphemisms may also be used in respect of certain historical incidents, and these may require intervention during translation: for example, whereas German scholars prefer to refer to the November Pogrom of 1938 (a notorious incident where Jewish were attacked by German Nazis), English texts might render it using the more expressive German term *Kristallnacht*, or its direct translation 'Crystal Night' or 'Night of Broken Glass', because the incident is not deemed to be particularly sensitive to English readers (Brown 2015: 14). To make decisions of this nature, the translator cannot remain at the level of what the text says, but must research the possible nuances lurking behind the surface level of the language.

Translational interventions may also be called for when the identity of the end-user changes as a text crosses cultural borders. An academic text intended for a lay audience will probably not include meticulous footnotes or a full bibliography. But when this text is translated to be published by a university press – which means its readers are likely to be specialists or semi-specialists – more extensive source information may need to be added. Text type and skopos are both relevant considerations here. What is the nature of the text I am about to translate? Who will be reading my translation and what is the object of their reading (recreation, scholarly studies, etc.)? What are the marketing concerns of the publisher? These questions all come to bear on the translator's textual decisions.

There is also the more technical issue of quotations in the ST cited from other foreign-language sources (not in the TL). Brown (2015: 13) recommends that the translator in this case would need to track down published or authoritative translations of those foreign sources in the TL, rather than translate them directly from the SL. Library or archival research would be inevitable. And what if in the course of research, the translator finds errors in the ST? Brown maintains that even though the translator is not explicitly charged with the task of fact-finding, it is entailed in the research process. She recommends pointing out the identified errors to the authors and publishers, who 'are always appreciative when mistakes are discovered, so my resulting questions generally increase their trust in and respect for my work' (14). This again demonstrates that the translator is not working in isolation, but in *translaboration* with other parties in the chain of production, thus turning translation into translatorial action.

Our second example is a case of self-translation by Judith Samuel, author of *The City of Ottawa*, a book on Victorian maritime history. Samuel is commissioned by a publisher in Quebec to self-translate her book into French within six months. Functionalist theories apply here, because Samuel is not performing translation for its own sake; there is a commissioner and a brief, and the book is intended for consumption by a particular audience. Although a professional researcher, Samuel does not have comprehensive knowledge of sailing; in her English text she quotes authorities in English 'without necessarily understanding every word' (Samuel 2014: 24). This might work in the original, especially if targeting an academic readership, but becomes a problem in translation: anyone who has dabbled in translation knows it is impossible to translate something you do not thoroughly understand.

To complete the project, Samuel has to do more than translate her own words; she needs to do research, this time in the capacity of a translator: 'A great resource was the book on Quebec historic shipbuilding by Eileen Reid Marcil, the leading authority in the field ... This provided vocabulary for the technical aspects of shipbuilding, for instance with regard to materials ... and construction' (24); 'I used the 1889 edition of *Nautical Terms in English and in French* to ensure the vocabulary was authentically in period' (25).

And when published resources fail her, Samuel resorts to human expertise and the internet: 'I could not find "laying tide rode" in any dictionary. A nautical friend, Pat Longfield ... explained that this meant the vessel was anchored at one end, so that it was swinging on its mooring following the tides. By some creative use of the Larousse online dictionary, I discovered that the French word was *évitage*' (25). Brown's and Samuel's examples illustrate the kind of due diligence a professional translator should be prepared to undertake, namely, researching beyond the perimeters of the original text, and also interacting with the author and publisher. This is part and parcel of the larger communicative event of book publishing, and should be regarded as the duty of a translator as translatorial actor.

Translation as genetic transfer

We mentioned earlier in relation to translatorial action that translation adds value to the circulation of goods and services in the commercial world. George Ho, an experienced translator based in New Zealand, provides two illustrative examples. Both cases deal with advertisements, which, as you will recall, are archetypically operative in the terms of text-type theory. To translate an operative text well, a translator goes for its effect, sometimes at the total expense of the words. Working on the understanding that 'the key to successful production of a quality translation of any advertising material is knowledge of appropriate culture-based marketing strategies in the business world and of consumer psychology and behaviour' (Ho 2004: 227), Ho adeptly demonstrates how faithfulness and creativity need not contradict each other in translation.

The first case example is that of a marketing campaign promoting a certain brand of kiwifruit. The English original is simple: 'This is the world's finest kiwifruit./New Zealand kiwifruit./Superior colour, texture, size, freshness, and, most importantly, taste.' At the level of language, these lines are very translatable. The question is: would a direct transfer of the text fulfil the skopos of this particular commission, which ultimately is to *add value* to the sales of the kiwifruit? Such functionalist thinking is pertinent especially in the case where the product being advertised is an unfamiliar commodity in the target market. Considering that prospective Chinese consumers may not be able to identify with the various characteristics (colour, texture, size, taste) of the New Zealand kiwifruit as described in the ST, Ho decides to extract the essence of each line and recontextualise it in a way that would appeal to his target audience. The following is a literal back-translation of the Chinese TT:

This is the fruit from Heaven to people on earth
Chinese gooseberry from New Zealand.
Jade green in colour, a pulp as soft as crisp candy,
With a size not too big, not too small,
With a wonderfully sweet taste and a smell as lovely as the Chinese rice wine's,
An integral whole with colour, smell and taste.

(Ho 2004: 231–232)

At first sight, it might seem that the translator has taken way too much liberty with the ST; upon closer inspection, however, we find that the core idea of each line in the ST is reproduced not in its original wording, but in an extrapolative and elaborated linguistic form that sneaks in cultural imagery evoking a familiar sense of Chineseness. Metaphorically speaking, those core ideas constitute the 'genetic codes' of the ST, and would need to be modified and transplanted in the TL to create a 'transgenic text or message' (Ho 2004: 228). Thus the idea of being the world's finest fruit (Line 1 in the ST) is now 'fruit from Heaven to people on earth' in the Chinese version, which conveys the same meaning using the idiomatic phrase *renjian xianguo* (literally 'heavenly fruit on earth'). The word 'kiwifruit' in Line 2 of the ST is now 'Chinese gooseberry' (*mihou tao*); the gooseberry, which is indigenous to China and later brought to New Zealand, is the predecessor of the kiwifruit, which justifies this lexical substitution.

The third line of the ST is rendered in a rhythmic series of four-character expressions imbued with rich imagery, with its 'genes' kept intact: thus 'superior colour' becomes 'the colour of jade' (*se ru feicui*); '(superior) texture' becomes '(a pulp) as soft as crisp candy' (*rang ru sutang*); '(superior) size' becomes 'a size not too big, not too small' (*da xiao shizhong*); and '(superior) taste' becomes 'a wonderfully sweet taste and a smell as lovely as the Chinese rice wine's' (*weigan xiangchun*). This technique creates a sort of Chinese jingle that evokes a palpable sensuousness, enhancing the desirability of the product. To repackage the kiwifruit into a desirable entity is indeed the motivation for the major shifts performed in this translation. These shifts can be rationalised by recourse to the functionalist paradigm, which looks at translation as a purposeful activity with a specific goal and participating in a value-driven process – in this case the marketing of a fruit commodity to increase its sales in the target market.

The second example is that of a video script for a TV tourist advertisement promoting Singapore as a preferred destination. This is yet another excellent illustration of the extent to which a ST can be manipulated to achieve its skopos, in this case to enhance the attractiveness of Singapore as a tourist destination. In line with this skopos we need a set of criteria, and this time we have a commission. This takes the form of specific instructions from the copywriter to the translator: to render the translation 'funky' and 'slick', and to afford it an 'edge' or 'layering' (Ho 2004: 235).

As with the previous example, there is nothing untranslatable about the ST in itself – the language is simple, straightforward, and not loaded with culture-specific items. But while the text is translatable at the level of language, the functionalist translator should be concerned with something extraneous to the individual expressions and structures: whether the

TT can materialise the intended effects of sounding funky, slick, edgy, and layered as stated in the commission. The translator George Ho discusses his strategy with reference to the genetic metaphor mentioned earlier:

> proceeded to apply the 'genetic engineering' strategy by extracting the key points of the USP [Unique Selling Proposition] of Singapore as the genetic codes of the original. Then I 'modified' or 'manipulated' these 'codes' to make the new hybrid translation appeal to potential Chinese viewers by foregrounding the traditional value of Chinese culture while keeping the USP of Singapore as background support. In other words, while retaining "the subject of discourse" of the advertisement, I strategically modified what Simon Anholt calls "the mode of discourse", namely, the verbal communication "flexibly tailored to the varying needs of the consumer" ... to produce an effective translation.
>
> (Ho 2004: 236)

A juxtaposition of the original English script and its Chinese version back-translated into English reveals the 'genetic engineering' procedure adopted by the translator:

English ST	Back-translation from the Chinese TT
I want to be where the world comes to play.	People all say, Singapore is a shining jewel in the crown of the South Pacific Ocean...
Incentive Isle Singapore.	Oh, Singapore, the dream of the South Pacific Ocean.
Gateway to Asia.	The Window to Asia.
I want the past.	With a rich tradition, With a lustrous culture.
I want the present.	With modern tastes, With trendy fashions.
I want to be dazzled.	I want to get drunk tonight, I want to get drunk in the South Pacific.
I want to taste heaven.	Bring me delicious food, Bring me best wines.

I want to be among the stars.	I want to dance with stars, I want to be a company of the moon.
I want to be a party animal.	I want to get lost in the fiesta, I want to enjoy myself tonight.
I want to shop, shop, shop.	I want to buy all the goods with brand names, Which are so attractively displayed.
I want to be pampered.	Be treated as a king. Be spoiled as a queen.
I want to explore.	I want to discover. I want to explore.
Incentive Isle Singapore.	Oh, Singapore, the dream of the South Pacific Ocean.

Source: (Ho 2004: 233–234, 237)

The Chinese translation uses radically different verbal formulations than the English original. New images are installed: in Line 7, the figurative 'taste heaven' in the English becomes the more literal food and wine in the Chinese; in Line 8, the image of stars in the ST is extended to stars and moons in the TT. The translator also adds a familiar musical rhythm to the Chinese version by extensively deploying parallel sets of four-character expressions. So is the translation faithful? This question is not nuanced enough to be answered adequately, for we must first ask: faithful to what? Surely the translator has distanced himself from the original copy both lexically and structurally. But despite this deviation in form, the translation manages to capture the core message (or the Unique Selling Proposition, mentioned in the quote above) of each corresponding line in the ST. It further seeks to add value to the marketing campaign by 'appeal[ing] to viewers' fantasy about this dreamland [Singapore] and even creat[ing] a touch of nostalgia' (Ho 2004: 136), most notably in the use of the word *nanyang* ('south seas'), an obsolete appellation used by overseas Chinese communities in Southeast Asia.

For example, the expression 'I want to be a party animal' is expanded into the octosyllabic *jinge kuangwu, le zai qi zhong*. This literally means 'to sing and dance to one's heart's content; to immerse oneself in fun', and seems to have over-translated the propositional content of the ST – being a party animal. But if we think about it carefully, isn't partying ultimately about singing, dancing, and enjoying oneself? Has the translation substantively altered anything? Or is it just 'stretching' the ST? Similarly, the line 'I want to be pampered' is reimagined in a way that can resonate with target Chinese audiences by invoking images of an imperial lifestyle from the ancient past: *diwang fengfan* ('in the style of emperors and kings'), *guifei chongyu* ('to receive the favours bestowed to an imperial consort'). The stylistic flamboyance of the Chinese words and structures richly conveys a sense of indulgence, which ties in with the idea of being pampered in the original.

In fact, if we work through this example closely, comparing the ST and TT line for line, we see that the translation extends or reconfigures the original formulations while carefully adhering to the theme of each line; for example: 'past' (Line 4) → 'tradition' + 'culture'; 'present' (Line 5) → 'tastes' + 'fashions', and so on. On the level of its surface manifestation, then, the translation seems to have transformed the ST considerably, but in fact this is not an all-out rewrite but a creative and calculated transposition. It is highly performative in its structure but also eminently faithful to the propositions in the original.

This is nearly a paradox – the translation is so far yet so close to the original. A functionalist view enables us to appreciate how the translator is striving to reproduce the genetic code – the DNA of the text, if you will – in a modified linguistic form that is digestible to the target consumer. Just as genes mutate as they travel from one physical body to another, so the DNA of a ST transfigures itself as it moves into the linguistic body of a TT, even propagating itself in multiple TTs, each with its unique configuration of essentially the same foundational DNA. The genetic metaphor is in alignment with the functionalist paradigm, and can serve as a kind of heuristic to think about what transpires when one translates for function as opposed to equivalence.

Localisation

Texts move. Virtually they move by being translated from one language into another, by incarnating themselves in another text existing in another culture. As artefacts, texts can also migrate in a more corporeal way across a spatial-temporal domain, where they are 'material objects that are constantly being distributed in time and space, just as material subjects (people) are' (Pym 2004: 5). To Anthony Pym, this 'very material kind of distribution' involving 'a set of real movements through time and space' underpins a process called **localisation**: the perpetual disseminating of texts, including such things as software and video games, across locales, languages, and cultures.

An anecdotal example cited by Pym is illustrative. The text in question is an English-language advertisement inviting participation in a tender in Kuwait, published in the French newspaper *Le Monde*, with a gist translation of the content into French. It was read by Pym who happened to be in Madrid at the time. Pym constructs a hypothetical trajectory for the advertisement as follows:

> Texts were moving. Perhaps a [Kuwaiti] prince or minister's verbal reply to a question became an internal memo, then re-drafted by a finance department, sent through various hands in an external relations department, converted into publicity copy. Production itself surely involved complex distribution. Eventually, let us imagine, this multi-authored advertisement was sent from the Kuwaiti Ministry of Public Works to an international agent (where? in London?), then to newspapers all over the world. But also, later, in that sleepless hotel in Madrid, the announcement was still moving through time, relentlessly approaching the closing date ... And even now, if you think about it, that text is still moving, through time if not through space, as is the one you are reading at the moment. And we too are in movement. *This is a world of moving texts and people, objects and subjects.*
>
> (Pym 2004: 8; emphasis added)

And if we may add to that last statement – languages as well. For Pym, 'real movement' refers to the transferring and traversing of a material text along a trail and within a distribution network emanating from its point of genesis, and this movement often entails crossing all kinds of borders: national, ethnic, cultural, and of course linguistic. Localisation, which involves textual translation and semiotic transfiguration, is conditioned by such movement.

Watch this clip

Using the links provided below, watch a video lecture on YouTube (in two parts) by Anthony Pym on theories of localisation. Before you watch this, think through the following questions and keep them in mind as you listen to what Pym has to say about localisation.

1. How would you characterise the movement of ideas and technologies between centres and peripheries in the global economy? How does such movement impact on the directionality of translation?

2. Is translation a key component within the workflow of localisation projects, or is it a 'bolt' that supports other (more important) processes within the chain? What is Pym's view on this point? And what is *your* view?

3. 'In this world, translation has evolved into a lot more asymmetrical things', Pym tells us. Do you think we still need the term 'localisation'; or do you think the expanded form of the term 'translation' can encapsulate the phenomenon in question?

4. 'People only know translation and localisation exist when they go wrong.' What is your opinion on this statement?

5. What kinds of minutiae need to be attended to in localisation?

Links
Part 1: www.youtube.com/watch?v=DkP5i3ve2cs
Part 2: www.youtube.com/watch?v=En1daH6MCDw

As a generic term, localisation refers to the act of embedding a foreign entity into an indigenous sociocultural framework, in the course of which certain features of the entity are adjusted to accommodate its new setting. As a technical term, it denotes an emerging service industry that is the product of global capitalism. With economic globalisation, commodities and services circulate vigorously across languages and cultures around the planet; and because languages and cultures are inherently different from one another, this circulation requires mediation. This mediation process is encapsulated in the acronym **GILT**, which stands for: Globalisation, Internationalisation, Localisation, Translation.

We might unpack GILT as follows: in a *globalised* economy, profit-driven companies would want to *internationalise* their products or services beyond the borders of their place of origin; to introduce their products or services seamlessly into a foreign market operating under a different linguistic and cultural background, companies need to *localise* them, meaning to adapt the products or services to the local circumstances. As language is almost always involved, either as an inherent part of the product or service, or in the course of its sales and marketing, we often need to *translate* as we localise. This has been well-recognised in the drinks industry, where translation is instrumental to international marketing communication: Heineken, for example, runs advertising campaigns in English and Spanish, even featuring the Puerto Rican actor Benicio Del Toro to capture the demographically significant Hispanic market in the USA and Latin America (Chartered Institute of Linguists 2016: 22–23).

In a nutshell GILT is an intermediary, **multimodal intervention** to facilitate the migration of a product/service from the point of origin to the point of destination. It is fundamentally about companies repackaging their products and services to appeal to specific locales, and is most frequently associated with websites, video games, software, or other digital platforms, though as a general phenomenon it need not be restricted to technological products and e-commerce.

Imagine a multinational retail company with stores all over the world. This company would need to produce websites, press releases, and catalogues (both electronic and hard copies) in different languages to cater to consumers all over the world. It may also need to change the colour coding of its local websites, social media platforms or apps it uses for promotion (depending on which platform/app is predominant in the target market), as well as currencies and measurements. Different images and taglines may need to be used in marketing brochures or banners to speak to the cultural sensibilities of the target market. These are all formations of verbal and nonverbal target text that dovetail into crosscultural marketing.

For example, the British beverage company Innocent has its website in 14 different versions, the visual designs of which are not identical across the board. As we might expect, there is always a textual element that needs to be negotiated: in one advertising campaign, the word pun in the English tagline 'Say hello to innocent's new squeeze', where 'squeeze' means both the act of making juice and 'boyfriend'/'girlfriend', is adapted into the French *Pressé avec amour* ('squeezed with love'). The twist comes in the form of the footnote *jus-ré*, suggesting *juré* ('I promise'; 'I swear'); this is a kind of 'innocent-speak' that children say to each other, hence resonating with the mood of the original tagline (and also the product name Innocent) in a subtle way (Reynolds 2016: 39–42).

Localisation as multimodal intervention

Localisation is a multimodal intervention in the sense that it deals with different kinds of sign simultaneously, including the verbal (texts), the visual (images), and even the aural (sounds) in the case of TV advertising. It can be seen as a value-driven mode of adaptation that serves the needs of corporate and commercial sectors, although the concept can be used more generally in non-corporate, non-commercial settings as well.

We shall be speaking of this phenomenon as localisation, for this term alone captures the whole process of GILT: it implies globalisation and internationalisation, and subsumes translating as an instrument. Localisation exemplifies translatorial action. In the localisation industry, translation constitutes part of language solutions (explained earlier) offered to businesses to help them proliferate their goods and services internationally. In a typical language solutions package, there are other component tasks that require expert skills and knowledge, such as software programming, technological adaptation, web design, and typesetting. In this professional setup, translation (proper) does not play its own game; it contributes its resources to a larger game that culminates not merely in a tangible textual product, but in a crosscultural campaign.

Localisation is about the degree of *situatedness* of a product or service. Achieving situatedness involves more than just translating a tagline idiomatically into the TL – that is one level, the linguistic level. Other modalities come into play: images in the original may need substitutions to correspond to the realities of the TL world, or to avoid inadvertent allusions to offensive issues. Localisation is thus about blending, or better still, *insinuating* a piece of communication into the cultural frame of the TL, which requires meticulous attention to semiotic details – both verbal and nonverbal.

When books and movies travel

Do you know that when books and movies 'travel' into other languages and cultures via translation their titles can metamorphose into something quite different? Titles are relatively short, so why can't we translate them as they are, as per the equivalence paradigm? The answer is that it is not just the title we are translating, but the concept of the book or movie as embodied in the title. On this view, the unit of translation is not the particular phrase or expression that constitutes the title, but the commodity as a whole. Whether a title should be literally translated, mildly adapted, or completely rewritten is more of a marketing than a stylistic consideration, and this is usually how language practices participate in the chain of product circulation.

Sometimes a book's title is localised in a foreign market simply because a literal translation would sound unpalatable. This is not just a linguistic concern: the sales of the book are at stake, for it is through its title that a prospective reader first comes into contact with a book. Michael Lewis's book *Boomerang* is about the global credit bubble that will eventually 'hit back' at major debtor nations, hence the boomerang metaphor. The metaphor, apt as it is in English, may or may not work in other languages, especially non-European languages. In Chinese, translating the word 'boomerang' literally would be very problematic, as the Chinese equivalent (*huifei bang*) has a morpheme for 'stick' (*bang*) at the end, which gives it a very literal texture, that is, it can only refer to the physical object, offering limited potential for metaphorical extension. This explains why the Chinese version for Lewis's book opts for an idiomatic explication of the book's theme: 'To become the victim of one's deeds' (*Zi shi e guo*), though this is strictly speaking a lexicalised metaphor in Chinese.

A book title should always be translated with regard to the theme of the book, which puts it in the functionalist rather than equivalence paradigm. Hence, James Macdonald's book *When Globalization Fails* becomes 'The Unease/Insecurity of Big Countries' (*Da guo de bu an*) in Chinese. At first sight this seems gratuitous, as it is completely possible for the original title to be rendered much more closely on the level of the language. But in assessing the quality of this translation, we really need to look beyond the title itself and have recourse to the content of the book. Part of the book's blurb reads:

> James Macdonald stresses that if industrial nations are more prosperous, they are also more vulnerable. While a dependence on trade may push toward cooperation, the attendant *insecurity* pulls in the opposite direction, leading to conflict. Today, the Pax Americana that kept *insecurities* at bay is being *undermined* by China's rise, with potentially dangerous consequences.
>
> (Macdonald 2015; emphasis added)

Combined with the subtitle 'The Rise and Fall of Pax Americana', this blurb highlights the interrelated themes of insecurity, impermanence, and vulnerability. The word *bu an* ('unease'; 'insecurity') in the Chinese translation speaks directly to the thematic thrust of the book, notwithstanding its apparent deviance from the English title. Using our genetic metaphor, the DNA of the English book has been translated through a mutation of the form of its title.

The same logic applies to the translation of movie titles. Hollywood movies travel all around the world, but they don't always bear the same title. There are varying degrees to which the original English titles are adhered to. In Anglophone territories they would most likely be retained; in non-Anglophone regions, they may be rendered more or less literally into the local language, or they could be entirely rewritten to accommodate the linguistic habits of the receiving culture. We might propose the following hypothesis in respect of movie titles as well as other kinds of text of a similar nature: *the stronger the cultural identity of a locale, the higher the degree of localisation.* In Hong Kong, for example, the titles of

Try this

Consider the title of the book *UnMarketing: Everything Has Changed and Nothing Is Different*, by Scott Stratten and Alison Stratten. Suppose you were asked to translate the book's title into another language of your choice. How would you go about doing it? Try the following steps:

1. Find a synopsis or review of the book online. If at all possible, browse through the book quickly to get a gist of it.
2. Think of a concise formulation to encapsulate the DNA of the book.
3. Consider whether the English title is marked, and if so, what rhetorical features have been put in place.
4. Translate the book's title literally into another language of your choice. Consider the efficacy of your literal translation in terms of marketing communication, bearing in mind that the skopos of your translation is to increase the sales figures of the translated book.
5. Assuming the literal translation does not work or is not the optimal choice, localise the book's title, having regard to its DNA. Consider how you may exploit nonverbal features to bring forth or even enhance the essence of the title.

Hollywood movies are heavily adapted almost to the point of rewriting, a phenomenon that is not attested in all Chinese-speaking regions.

Test out the validity of this hypothesis on a sample of translated movie titles in your culture, and see if the outcome accords with your understanding of the resilience or susceptibility to external influences of your culture or another culture with which you are familiar. Of course, in commercially driven contexts the ultimate concern is not culture but profits: the skopos of translation here is to facilitate and positively enhance marketing communication so as to boost the reception of a product or service.

Translation and global marketing communications: Apple Inc.

Let us look at a second case of localisation: the global advertising strategies of Apple Inc., with specific focus on Greater China – comprising mainland China (MC), Hong Kong (HK), and Taiwan (TW). We know of course that Apple Inc.'s official website has many local incarnations all over the world. What is interesting in the case of Greater China is that instead of one generic Chinese version used throughout the three Sinophone regions, there is a further tier of localisation, with variations built into the MC, HK, and TW versions. An advertisement in English can therefore be translated into more than one Chinese-language version, sometimes with significant differences.

But why do that? Wouldn't it be more cost-effective to simply use one version across all three Chinese regions? Since localisation is an investment, there must be sound reason for this. That reason is found in the differentiated use of the Chinese language within Greater China, which makes it a sophisticated case for our purpose here. Take, for example, the tagline for iPhone 7: 'This is 7.' The force of this tagline lies in its absolute simplicity, using the bare number 7 to stand in for the name of the model. It seems almost too easy to translate it into any language. And indeed the Chinese versions for the MC (back-translation: '7, is here') and TW (back-translation: 'Simply 7') versions reproduce the terse form of the English version.

The HK version, however, reads: 'This, is simply iPhone 7' in back-translation. Apart from the insertion of a comma after the Chinese word for 'This', the structure is also palpably longer; and it appears to have missed the rhetorical point of substituting '7' for 'iPhone 7', making the tagline less crisp than the original. This is not an instance of careless translation, but one of localisation. It so happens that in colloquial

Cantonese, the predominant Chinese dialect used in Hong Kong, the number 7 has a pejorative connotation. To describe someone's appearance as 'seven' means to say s/he looks old-fashioned, clumsy, or generally unpleasant, and this usage is deeply rooted in local parole.

Which means to say, a literal translation of 'This is 7' into Chinese will most certainly be interpreted by a local Hongkonger as 'This is old-fashioned' or 'This is clumsy' – obviously not the kind of association that iPhone 7 is supposed to invoke! Remember that when a native Hongkonger reads a Chinese tagline, s/he will be thinking in Cantonese, not Mandarin – what is called Standard Chinese. Thus, although we are speaking of what is ostensibly one language, to use the MC or TW translation in Hong Kong without regard of the subtle peculiarities of the local vernacular would have resulted in a faux pas. In the actual HK version, this is averted by attuning to the nuances of the Hong Kong dialect and neutralising the potentially adverse associations of a central signifier – in this case the number 7.

Mitsubishi Pajero/Montero/Shogun

The importance of attending to the sensitivities of language in global marketing communications can be demonstrated in an analogous example from the automobile industry. The Mitsubishi Pajero is a Japanese SUV model, so named presumably because *pajero* (after the Pampas cat *Leopardus pajeros* indigenous to parts of Latin America) invokes exotic overtones for Japanese consumers.

Rather unfortunately, *pajero* means 'wanker' in Spanish – a nuance neither Mitsubishi nor its drivers would want to be attached to. Which probably explains why the same model is known instead as the Montero (*montero*, literally 'mountain huntsman') in most of Latin America and also in the USA, where Spanish speakers are in the millions.

Interestingly, in the UK the model is marketed as the Shogun, a Japanese word referring to the chief military leader in feudal Japan, thus bringing the car model full circle to its culture of origin – though not in its own land. Apparently people tend to see the cultural Other as enticingly exotic, and here we witness how this pervasive psychology is exploited through the localisation of brand names in multilingual marketing.

Linguistic manoeuvres are especially crucial in the negotiation of humour across cultures. In an advertisement for iOS stickers, the US, MC, HK, and TW versions present interesting divergences. Each image is a screenshot of a messaging app with a riddle text on it. The English original reads: 'Why can't a nose be twelve inches long?/Because then it'll be a foot.' None of the Chinese versions is a direct translation of the English, and this is in itself a clever translation strategy. In Chinese, the word for 'foot' (unit of measurement) creates no pun with 'foot' (part of a leg), so the English word play would have been lost in translation.

What is more remarkable is this: each of the three Chinese versions develops its own unique riddle tapping into a linguistic point that resonates with a specific repertoire. The MC version uses the morpheme *ya* in the word for 'feet' (*jiaoya*) to pun with the word for 'duck' (*ya*); the HK version plays with the homophone *suk*, which can mean 'cooked' (as in food) or 'close' (as in between friends); and the TW version uses a local food item *binlang* (betel nut) and homophonises it into the pseudo-compound 'ice-wolf' (read *bing-lang*) to create a joke about a wolf falling into icy water. Even with my translational expositions here, the English reader would fail to find the Chinese versions humorous. And that should indeed be the case, for otherwise these riddles would have lost their linguistic and cultural specificity. The untranslatability of humour is thus the motivation behind the efforts taken to adapt the riddle to its specific readership. Even though the point of this advertisement is more about the stickers than the content of the messages, the texts are nevertheless still subject to careful crosscultural treatment, which suggests that in localisation, texts are seen as *gestalts*, that is, as holistic visual-discursive objects.

Orthographic and visual manipulations further demonstrate the intricate semiotic processes at work. Each of the Chinese versions uses a different script: the simplified script for MC, the vernacular Cantonese script for HK, and the traditional script for TW. The user profile has changed: 'Brian' in the English version is 'translated' into Chinese names and faces; and while the HK and TW versions use the same person, the MC version differentiates itself by using a different Chinese face and name. This 'translation' of Western identities into Asian ones for the Greater Chinese market is not uncommon in Apple Inc.'s advertising campaigns.

What this kind of transposition demonstrates is that localisation can involve a thorough **resemiotisation** (the reconfiguration of signs), in which visuality is a salient factor. The most illustrative example of such translation in marketing communication can be found in the advertisement 'Switching to iOS from Android is easy'. Comparing the US and MC versions, we see that the app icons on the respective screens are quite different. The MC version substitutes several of the apps found in the US version that are not applicable to the local situation in mainland China, including Facebook, Twitter, Lyft, Instagram, and Snapchat. The screen on the MC version features instead popular apps uniquely relevant to its social culture, such as *Tianmao*, *Taobao* (both shopping apps), *Dazhong dianping* (a lifestyle app), *Kaixin xiao xiao le* (a game app), *Zhihu* (a popular Q&A app), and *Weixin* (WeChat, a messaging app). As marketing discourse is multimodal, such revisualisation should be viewed within the broader notion of translation-as-communication, alongside more conventional modes of semiotic transfer such as interlingual translation.

Successful localisation involves strategic manipulation of apparently minute details via both textual translation and semiotic reworking. The advertisement 'Nobody understands you quite like Siri' consists of an image with two overlapping screens. The screen on the right shows how one uses Siri to recall an earlier message: 'When is Karla's recital? Was she supposed to practice first?' sent to a certain John Bailey. The three Chinese translations retain basically the same question, with a minor variation in the MC and TW versions (which say in the second line: 'I guess she's started practising already'). Conspicuously, the names Karla and John Bailey are converted into common Chinese names. There is also intralingual translation, where the same question is crafted in slightly different forms: the HK version uses Cantonese as usual with its idiosyncratic lexis and dialectal script; and while the MC and TW versions are very similar, they use different lexical choices (*duzou yinyue hui* versus *yanzou hui* for '(solo) recital'; *na tian* versus *shenme shihou* for 'when'; *guji* versus *cai* for 'guess'). These choices presumably represent idiomatic usage in the respective linguistic communities, though we could also see this as an issue of register (see Chapter 4).

What is more interesting is the left screen. The English original features Lyft, a transportation company based in San Francisco, a snapshot of the direction map, and a Siri message that reads: 'Lyft can be there in 3 minutes. Do you want to request it?' The MC version translates this message, except that Lyft is now changed to *Didi chuxing*, the dominant provider of car-sharing services in mainland China. The geographical setting of the communication has also been changed to Beijing, with the direction map and message on the screen accordingly transposed. If we were operating at the level of language alone, we would call this dynamic equivalence; but here we are dealing with a real-world entity, so it is less about linguistic equivalence than it is about constructing an equivalent semiotic response to the local circumstance, but the idea of dynamism is nonetheless the same.

The HK and TW versions are quite different; they illustrate using Siri to schedule the day's activities rather than to order car services. This shift must have been a calculated one, because, at least at the time of the advertisement, there were no equivalent car-sharing service companies legally registered in either Hong Kong or Taiwan, which makes Lyft irrelevant to these two locales. This is analogical to the notion of a lexical/ semantic gap at the level of language; the gap here is not linguistic in nature but the arising issue is similar. The solution adopted here is to circumvent the locale-specific item (Lyft) by substituting a more generic operation (scheduling of activities). This is a form of translational compensation, albeit not at a textual level but at the level of the entire visual-discursive frame. And here, an impressive degree of care is taken to effect another level of localisation in the HK and TW versions: the same activity 'drink coffee with Shu Ling' at 10.30 a.m. takes place at different places – Coco Expresso and Amay Teahouse, which are actual cafés in real-world Hong Kong and Taiwan respectively.

To conclude: how do we fit localisation into the frame of translation studies, or conversely, translating into the bigger picture of localisation as a mode of communication? In each of the previous examples from Apple Inc., we are working with different local versions of same advertisements; these various versions function autonomously in their respective markets, which means they are instrumental translations. Following Christiane Nord (see earlier section on skopos theory), instrumental translations are focused on the effect rather than the formal constitution of the ST. In the case of localisation, texts are designed and translated to maximise marketing effect in different linguistic and cultural territories, and to achieve this purpose, the form (both discursive and visual) of the translated-localised texts may need to be adapted, transmuted, and metamorphosed into one that the TL market can fully assimilate.

Try this

On your browser, open two language versions of Apple Inc.'s official website, the US version and one other version of your choice. (You can adapt this exercise by choosing other mobile technology conglomerates such as Samsung, or by comparing three language versions instead of two.)

Choose any product and browse through its advertisements on both websites in parallel. Can you find interesting divergences between two language versions of the same advertisement? Can you explain possible motivations behind such divergences in terms of localisation? Use our preceding discussion on the iOS examples as a reference.

Further reading and reflection

1. Read the following article by Christiane Nord: 'Loyalty and Fidelity in Specialized Translation', *Confluências. Revista de Tradução Científica e Técnica* 4: 29–41 (2006). The article can be accessed via this link: http://web.letras. up.pt/egalvao/TTCIP_Nord%20loyatly%20and%20fidelity.pdf
   a. How does Nord differentiate between the notions of fidelity and loyalty? Do you think this differentiation is one of reasonable substance?
   b. To what extent is it possible for a translator to be simultaneously 'loyal' to the ST author and the TT reader? Can you think of an example where this would be practically impossible?

2. Read the following article by Ira Torresi: 'Advertising: A Case for Intersemiotic Translation' (*Meta* 53[1]: 62–75, 2008). The article is available for free download via this link: www.erudit.org/revue/meta/2008/v53/n1/ 017974ar.pdf
   a. On p. 71, Torresi describes the 'text production chain' in advertising translation and the translator's position within this chain. How would you paraphrase the author's argument using the terms of translatorial action we have learnt in this chapter?
   b. Based on the examples in the article and its idea of intersemiotic translation, how would you characterise the relationship between verbal and nonverbal elements in advertising translation? To what extent do you think visual elements need to be translated across cultures?

3. Read a book chapter by Anthony Pym, entitled 'Website Localization' (Pym 2011), published in *The Oxford Handbook of Translation Studies*. A preprint version of the article is available at: http://usuaris.tinet.cat/apym/on-line/translation/2009_website_localization_feb.pdf

    a. What does website localisation reveal about the relation between technology and translation?

    b. Focusing on the websites of multinational conglomerates, to what extent do you think translation participates in and contributes to economic globalisation?

4 The Discourse Paradigm

Topic Map

TEXT STRUCTURE

- Key author: Mona Baker (1953–)
- Representative work: *In Other Words*
- Theory/model: Languages behave differently in respect of thematic patterning, markedness, information structure, cohesion, and coherence. In cases where direct transfer of textual links is not possible or desirable, translators generally need to rework the text structure of the SL to conform to TL conventions.

REGISTER ANALYSIS

- Key authors: Basil Hatim (1947–) and Ian Mason (1944–)
- Representative works: *Discourse and the Translator*; *The Translator as Communicator*
- Theory/model: The register of a text is determined by its Field (subject matter), Tenor (writer/speaker-reader/listener relationship), and Mode (written/spoken/multimodal). A text can be placed along a static-dynamic continuum, depending on whether it effects stable or turbulent communication. Generally speaking, a translation should be pegged at the same register and exhibit the same static/dynamic disposition as the original text.

TRANSLATION QUALITY ASSESSMENT

- Key author: Juliane House (1942–)
- Representative work: *Translation Quality Assessment*
- Theory/model: The quality of a translation can be assessed using the following methodology: (1) generate the ST register profile; (2) identify the genre of the ST as generated by its register; (3) produce a 'statement of function' for the ST; (4) repeat the first three steps for the TT; (5) error identification; (6) make a 'statement of quality' of the TT.

Discourse: A plural concept

'Discourse' is one of the most frequently occurring words in scholarly writing in the humanities. It is also one marked by mind-boggling plurality: the word has come to take on so many varied senses that one can almost pass off using the word, sometimes ostentatiously, without even knowing the precise meaning in which it is employed.

To begin with linguistics, discourse at a most rudimentary level refers to any part of a text extending beyond the unit of the sentence. This definition immediately runs into trouble with contrastive linguistics and translation, because the sentence unit is by no means an unequivocal concept when we look at it across languages. In English, a sentence is nominally marked by a full stop; now even though this little black dot that we call a punctuation mark exists in many modern languages, in several of these, notably Asian languages, it does not have the exclusive prerogative of marking the conceptual boundary of a sentence.

In translating closely from English into these languages, a comma could very well replace an English full stop at the exact corresponding point in the 'sentence' and still sound idiomatic, even more so than would be the case if a full stop were to be used. What we call a run-on sentence in English (the juxtaposition of two well-formed sentences without a conjunction) is a perfectly unmarked pattern in some Asian languages. Obviously, this creates a potential pitfall when translating from these languages into English.

Still within the field of linguistics but incorporating the perspective of social semiotics (the study of signs in society), discourse invokes the sense of language-in-use, as opposed to language as an abstract structure, hence: **Discourse Analysis**. This line has been taken up by translation studies scholars. In their book *The Translator as Communicator*, Hatim and Mason (1997: 216) define discourse as '[m]odes of speaking and writing which involve social groups in adopting a particular attitude towards areas of socio-cultural activity (e.g. racist discourse, bureaucratese, etc.)'. Here we can see a sociopsychological perspective entering into the study of language and translation and, conversely, the embedding of linguistic texts into social relations and networks. The implication of this is that texts are no longer seen as isolated enclaves that generate meanings within themselves, and hence the translator's horizon can no longer be restricted to the verbal signifiers of the text:

> Seeing the meaning of texts as something which is negotiated between producer and receiver and not as a static entity, independent of human processing activity once it has been encoded, is, we believe, the key to an understanding of translating, teaching translating and judging translations.
>
> (Hatim & Mason 1990: 64–65)

Since the discourse approach, at least as defined by Hatim and Mason, contributes 'to an understanding of translating, teaching translating and judging translations', it clearly serves a prescriptive function. Note, however, that this approach is also appropriated by later theorists (not least Hatim and Mason themselves) in a critical, non-prescriptive way, to uncover the ideological operations lurking beneath discursive choices – the calculated selection of which words or structures to use – in translation. In this specific sense, the definition of discourse tends toward the **Foucauldian**, and concerns institutional values and beliefs that regulate social behaviour. This line of study is concerned not with the linguistics of translating nor with the ultimate quality of a piece of translation, but with the political or ideological implication of an act of translation. Hence, it belongs to the domain of conceptual translation studies.

For now let us concentrate on what is happening within the text itself. Rather than focus on how individual expressions are rendered or how the text is actually put into use, we are now interested in how a translator approaches a text as an *organic entity* with an *internal economy* (i.e., with a structural logic of its own). This positions us between the equivalence and functionalist paradigms, that is to say, beyond a discrete unit of language (word, phrase, clause, idiom, etc.), but still within the physical perimeters of the material text – as opposed to emplacing the text within a functional chain of translatorial actions.

Within the discourse paradigm in translation, the guiding theoretical framework is **Systemic Functional Linguistics** (SFL). SFL is pioneered by the renowned linguist M. A. K. Halliday, and for that reason is sometimes known as Hallidayan linguistics. SFL is a major school in linguistics that works on the premise that language structure emerges through actual usage; this is diametrically opposite to the premise held by its competing school – Transformational-Generative Grammar (or Chomskyan linguistics, named after its pioneer Noam Chomsky) – that language structure is part of our innate faculty as human. SFL is a complicated framework, with entire books devoted to it. Translation theorists have tapped into different aspects of SFL, and this chapter looks at three salient applications: **text structure** (thematic and information patterning, cohesion, and coherence), **register** (static versus dynamic language), and **translation quality assessment**.

The structure of texts: Baker's analysis

Thematic patterning

In her acclaimed book *In Other Words*, Mona Baker draws on concepts from SFL to frame her discussion on issues in translating at the level of discourse. The first of these is thematic structure, which is central to Hallidayan linguistics. The **theme** refers to the first segment of a clause indicating what the clause is about. It connects backward to a prior stretch of text and forward to an ensuing stretch of text. The segment of the clause that comes after the theme is the **rheme**, which provides information about the theme and communicates the point of the utterance.

Hence in the utterance 'Jason went to the market', 'Jason' is the theme (grammatically it is the Subject), and the predicate that follows it is the rheme. The problem for translation is that different languages may employ different thematic patterns, that is, they can select different kinds of word to go into the theme position for a given stretch of text. When this happens, the translator would need to step in to mediate the difference to maintain a logical flow of ideas in the TL. Table 4.1 illustrates this with an example, based on Baker (2011: 139–141).

Markedness

Another related issue is that of **(un)markedness**. An item in a given sequence is *unmarked* if readers totally expect it to be there; on the other hand, it is *marked* if it appears slightly out of place or outright jarring, even though the entire sequence is perfectly grammatical. Translationese, a term that came up in Chapter 2, is an effect of a marked style in the

Table 4.1 Thematic patterning and translation

Issue	Implication for translating	Example
Theme and rheme sequencing	If the thematic patterning (selection of words in theme position for a given stretch of text) in the ST cannot be preserved in translation without affecting the grammaticality and/or acceptability of the TT, the translator should invoke an alternative thematic pattern to maintain a logical flow of information.	An English text uses the first-person pronoun 'I' in theme position frequently to maintain a coherent point of view (first-person). The thematic patterning foregrounds the speaker in the form: I, I, It, I, I, I, I, I, It, I. A French translation of this text would be able to keep the thematic structure: *Je, Je, Je, Je, Je, Je, J'ai, Je, La pire chose, Je*. An Arabic translation, however, cannot preserve the 'I' in theme position due to a fundamental grammatical difference: Arabic uses an inflected verb in theme position where a pronoun would be used in English. To maintain a sense of textual continuity, the translator has to change the thematic pattern to: *not-was, but-I, was-it, saw-I, saw-I, saw-I, occupied-I, since then, among the worst saw-I, pleases-me*. Here an 'ego-centric pattern' that works in English is preserved in French but replaced by a 'process-centric pattern' that works better in Arabic.

TL. In English, there are three instances where a theme becomes marked (Baker 2011: 141–149; examples mine):

1. by moving an item into the initial position of a clause, where it usually does not belong (**fronted theme**): 'Our students were squeezed into the tiny classroom' → '*Squeezed* into the tiny classroom were our students'
2. by using an *it*-structure (cleft structure) in the initial position (**predicated theme**): 'He went to Japan two years after the divorce' → '*It was two years after the divorce* that he went to Japan'
3. by using a *wh*-structure (pseudo-cleft structure) in the initial position (**identifying theme**): 'I want you to study real hard' → '*What I want* is for you to study real hard'

The problem for the translator is that an unmarked sequence in a SL can appear quite marked in the TL if directly transferred, and this is technically undesirable. Or: a marked sequence in a SL can appear *even more marked* in the TL – what is initially just mildly strange becomes obtrusively alien. To avoid this eventuality, the translator can intervene to tweak the thematic pattern. Table 4.2, based on Baker (2011: 149–151), illustrates this.

Table 4.2 Markedness and translation

Issue	Implication for translating	Example
Markedness	When the ST presents a marked sequence, it should be translated with an equally marked sequence in the TL.	An English text uses the *it*-structure in theme position, as in 'It is for such customers that ...'. This structure is much less marked in English than in German. When translating into German, the optimal method is to replace this with a more conventional theme: *Für solche Kunden* ('For such customers ...'). Similarly a *wh*-structure as theme sounds more strongly marked in Arabic than in English. Hence a clause beginning with 'What XXX wants ...' in English can be translated into Arabic along the line 'And seeks XXX ...'.

Information structure

Besides thematic structure, translators must consider how information is structured to ensure a good flow in the TT. One issue has to do with what is called **given** and **new information**. Given information is associated with the theme; it is that which is already known to the reader, either because it has been mentioned in prior discourse or because it forms part of the assumed background knowledge in that particular culture. New information is the main communicative point of an utterance, as conveyed by the rheme; it tells the reader something about the theme that s/he is not assumed to already know. The unmarked information structure is **given-before-new**; this correlates with the principle of **end-weight** in discourse, which dictates that heavier and lengthier segments are pushed toward the end of a sentence.

The problem for translation arises when these two principles contradict TL grammar. A translator must of course ensure that the TT is grammatically well-constructed, but in the course of doing so, s/he may inadvertently reverse the given-before-new and end-weight principles. Table 4.3 explains this with an example from Baker (2011: 157–158).

The idea of markedness, mentioned earlier, is also relevant to information focus. Different languages may have different conventions of signalling markedness. English uses typographical (e.g., italicisation) or punctuation devices. Baker's (2011: 167) example is the line 'The English have changed', where the underlined word is where the emphasis falls on (in speech, the same effect would be conveyed using tonal stress). A possible French translation is *Les Anglais, eux aussi, ont évolué*, which uses the word *eux aussi* ('as well') to emphasise *Les Anglais* ('The English'). Effectively, a lexical addition in the TT translates a typographical marker in the ST.

Cohesion: Reference, substitution/ellipsis, conjunction

Cohesion is an important component of Hallidayan linguistics. The term basically means how different parts of a text 'hang' together lexically or grammatically. In order for separate sentences to sound like an integral piece of discourse, certain devices need to be in place, so as to 'hook' one clause or sentence to another. In their classic work *Cohesion in English*, Halliday and Hasan (1976) identify five primary cohesive devices in English: reference, substitution, ellipsis, conjunction, and

Table 4.3 Information structure and translation

Issue	Implication for translating	Example
Given-before-new and end-weight principles	If the given-before-new and end-weight principles clash with TL grammatical principles, try to resolve the contradiction by applying certain procedures, such as switching between passive and active or inserting a weak subject.	Suppose we have an academic paper written in Brazilian Portuguese, which allows simple verbs to be fronted, e.g., *Foram estudados os efeitos de luz, de temperatura e dos tegumentos na germinação de sementes de limãocravo* (*Citrus limonia, Osb.*) ('Were studied the effects of light, of temperature and of presence/absence in germination of seeds of limão-cravo [Citrus limonia, Osb.]).
		A possible translation is this: 'The effects of light, temperature and the presence or absence of the seed coat on limão-cravo (Citrus limonia) seed germination have been studied.' In an attempt to conform to English grammar, the translator here sacrifices both the given-before-new and the end-weight principles: the new information, or what the reader really wants to know, is the thing being studied ('the effects of ...' – now fronted); the TT has a heavy subject ('The effects ...on seed germination'), with a short predicate ('have been studied'). One way to resolve this is to add a weak subject ('this paper' – given information) and switch the voice from passive to active: 'This paper examines the effects of light, temperature and the presence or absence of the seed coat on limão-cravo (Citrus limonia).'

lexical cohesion. The problem for translation is that different languages perform cohesion in different ways, and the above devices do not always work seamlessly across language pairs.

Let us begin with **reference**. In Halliday and Hasan's scheme, reference means how an entity mentioned in discourse is being referred to subsequently. Cohesion obtains where there is 'continuity of reference, whereby the same thing enters into the discourse a second time' (Halliday & Hasan 1976: 31). In English, for example, we use a personal pronoun to refer back to a noun mentioned within its co-text; this is called **pronominal reference**, which is a type of **anaphor** or pattern of reference. Baker (2011: 191) points out that languages 'that have number and gender distinctions in their pronoun system are less constrained in using this cohesive device, since different pronouns can be used to refer to different entities within a text with less possibility of confusion'.

For the translator, this means there is no universal way of establishing reference in discourse, and the translator must be sensitive to

---

Pronouns and address forms

Some Asian languages such as Thai have extremely complex pronominal systems, where the use of pronouns is contingent upon factors such as the relative age and social status of the interlocutors as well as their gender and the proximity of their relationship. Conceivably this would cause problems in English–Thai translation, as there are several options for 'I' and 'you' in Thai, differentiated by subtle nuances.

Thai speakers can additionally choose to address themselves and their interlocutors using other address forms, such as 'older brother/sister' (*phi*) and 'younger brother/sister' (*nong*). They can also use names, including using their own names to refer to themselves. Hence, if I am Tom and I'm talking to Jane, it is possible, depending on all the circumstances of the situation, to say something in Thai to the effect of 'Tom likes Jane' (*Tom chop Jane*), when what I really am saying is 'I like you'. Imagine the ludicrous outcome of transferring this Thai utterance straight into English, say, in a subtitle. The English viewer would be well justified in feeling confused as to whether another two persons are being referred to.

the differences between his/her working languages in respect to their unmarked or preferred patterns of reference. This is especially so when translating between distant languages.

A related concept is that of co-reference, which means using a related word or phrase (e.g., synonym, superordinate, general word) to refer back to an entity in discourse. For example, we might have the proper noun 'Oxford University' coming up in a text, and then being referred to again shortly afterward, but this time with the phrase 'the iconic institution'. This again poses a potential problem in translation, where connections that are obvious in the SL may instead cause rupture in the TL. Table 4.4 illustrates the implication of reference and co-reference for translating (based on Baker 2011: 193–196; Japanese and Chinese examples my own).

We can also use **substitution** and **ellipsis** to create cohesive links; these are not lexical but grammatical relations, as in: 'I'm getting a Coke. Do you want *one?*' (the word 'one' substitutes for 'a Coke') and 'A: You're really mean; B: Am I?' ('Am I?' is elliptic, truncated from 'Am I really mean?'). Once again, these may work well in some languages but not in others. Table 4.5 summarises this point with examples from Baker (2011: 198–199). It is interesting to compare this with Table 4.4: where pronominal reference is more preferred in English than in Brazilian Portuguese, it becomes a less preferred strategy when the counterpart language is Arabic.

Yet another cohesive device is **conjunction**, the use of connecting words between clauses, sentences, and paragraphs to create a sense of textual logic. Some languages use conjunctions more extensively than others to precisely and unambiguously signal syntactical relations. This recalls the traditional dichotomy between **hypotaxis** and **parataxis**. While English has been characterised as a hypotactic language with its frequent employment of conjunctions among other linking devices, Chinese, along with some other Asian languages, is often seen as a para-tactic language with loosely strung sentences, where the logical connec-tion between segments is often inferred from context rather than overtly indicated.

Following this, some English conjunctions can be reasonably dropped when translating into Chinese: 'I opened my handbag and found my wallet missing' becomes 'I opened ø handbag, ø found ø wallet missing' in Chinese. The comma in the middle technically substitutes the English

Table 4.4 Reference and translation

Issue	Implication for translating	Example
Reference	Depending on their grammatical properties, different languages have their own preferred means of tracing referents in discourse. The translator should adopt the pattern of reference conventionally used in the TL.	Where English favours lexical repetition, i.e., repeating the noun denoting the referent. For example, in referring back to proper nouns such as names, the convention in Brazilian Portuguese is to repeat the noun rather than use a pronoun.
		In Japanese and Chinese, where a grammatical subject is often omitted, pronominal reference is less frequently used than in English. When translating from English into these languages, at least some of the subject pronouns in the ST would need to be dropped. Consider two sentences: 'Jason went to the market. He bought a watermelon.' In Japanese and Chinese, the full stop demarcating the boundary of the two sentences can be removed, and the pronoun in the second sentence dropped to produce **zero-anaphora** (here a pronoun in absentia pointing backward to a precedent noun). The most idiomatic translation in Japanese and Chinese would be to the effect of 'Jason went to the market, bought a watermelon'.
Co-reference	A co-referent that is perfectly natural in the SL may sound awkward in the TL; in this case, the translator must intervene to change the pattern of reference, such as by lexical repetition or pronominal reference.	In the sentence 'None of the researchers have seen *the tigers*, but they know *the big cats* are lurking nearby', the two clauses are tied together by using 'big cats' to point back to 'tigers'. Translating 'big cats' literally into Chinese would at best result in an awkward reading and at worst mislead readers into suspecting there is a second referent other than 'the tigers'. Lexical repetition ('seen *the tigers*, but they know *the tigers* …') would be much preferred in Chinese. This technique works also because Chinese has a relatively high tolerance threshold for nominal repetition (see Table 4.7).

Table 4.5 Substitution/ellipsis and translation

Issue	Implication for translating	Example
Substitution and ellipsis	In the case where a substitution or ellipsis is not conventionally used in the TL, the translator must switch to another cohesive device.	In Arabic, verbs agree with their subjects in gender and number; cohesive links are thus built into the grammar, such that Arabic can make extensive use of pronominal reference without the risk of creating ambiguity. English, on the other hand, has few verbal inflections as compared to Arabic. Hence, when translating from Arabic, some pronouns would need to be dropped, and other interventions would need to be used, such as substitution, ellipsis, and lexical repetition. Thus, in 'if the authority which they agreed on nominating declines to appoint the arbitrator or is unable to nominate *him* within sixty days ...' (back-translated from Arabic), the pronominal reference 'him' is changed to 'one' in the English translation: 'if the nominated authority declines to appoint an arbitrator or is unable to nominate *one* within sixty days.'

conjunction, and splits 'and found ...' into a new clause. Notice that this clause has a zero subject, a case of zero-anaphora, pointing back to the subject 'I'; further: the pronominal adjective 'my' is twice elided in the Chinese. All of this speaks to the structural economy of Chinese vis-à-vis English. The hypotaxis-parataxis model has been criticised for being too simplistic, but it nevertheless signals the overarching tendencies of different languages in respect of textual connectivity in discourse. Table 4.6 describes the implication of conjunctions for translating, with an English–Arabic and an English–German example from Baker (2011: 201–210).

And then we have **lexical cohesion**, which is the relational network produced within a text through strategic selection of vocabulary. According to Halliday and Hasan (1976), the two relevant linguistic devices here are **reiteration** and **collocation**. Reiteration refers to the repetition of a lexical item in the same stretch of discourse, though the repeated word need not refer to the same entity as it does in its earlier occurrence. Collocation refers to the pairing of one lexical item with another; the actual relation between the two words within a collocation is immaterial, as long as they create a sense of textual unity. But some languages are more amenable to these devices than others, and translators need to negotiate the arising differences when translating between languages that do not behave in a similar way. There is also the issue of lexical gaps, where a SL word finds no direct replacement in the TL. Table 4.7 illustrates this with examples from Baker (2011: 216–220).

Cohesion: Multimodal discourse

A more complex type of cohesion is one that involves both verbal and nonverbal elements. An example from Baker (2011: 214) is illustrative: an advertisement for the magazine *Woman's Realm* features a woman wearing a large hat; the caption reads: 'If you think Woman's Realm is old hat ... think again.' Here the English idiom 'old hat', which describes something as uninteresting, creates a cohesive link with the picture of a hat in the visuals. If we were to translate this advertisement into a language where the 'old hat' idiom does not exist, we may need to change both the caption and the visuals in order to create a new cohesive link.

Table 4.6 Conjunctions and translation

Issue	Implication for translating	Example
Conjunction	The translator manages conjunctions in translation in a way that balances *accuracy* (by translating the SL conjunction closely) and *naturalness* (by using a TL conjunction or by dropping the conjunction altogether). The purpose of the translation would dictate the translator's inclination in this regard.	Arabic makes less frequent use of conjunctions than English, and many Arabic conjunctions need to be interpreted within the context of their utterance. In English-into-Arabic translation, translators often merge some sentences, and use typical, often less precise, Arabic conjunctions such as *wa* (roughly: 'and'), *fa* (rought: 'for') *hatha-wa* (literally: 'this and') and *kama* (roughly: 'also'/ 'in addition') to ensure naturalness. This is balanced by transferring some English conjunctions into Arabic to ensure accuracy. German makes more frequent use of conjunctions than English. In English-into-German translation, a translator may increase the number of conjunctions. But in practice, this also depends on the intended readership, because making a translation more conjunctive also makes it sound more formal.

Table 4.7 Lexical cohesion and translation

Issue	Implication for translating	Example
Lexical cohesion	Some languages such as Greek, Arabic, and Chinese have a higher tolerance threshold for reiteration than English; when translating from English into these languages, one might need to enhance lexical cohesion through increased lexical repetition.	A short extract from Stephen Hawking's *A Brief History of Time* displays a linguistic pattern where six lexical items are repeated as follows (number in brackets indicates frequency): *know* (2); *universe* (4); *time* (2); *answers* (2); *ridiculous* (2); *tower of tortoises* (2). The Spanish translation uses a similar pattern. By contrast, the Greek translation shows a higher number of items repeated and a higher frequency of repetition for some items: *anthropi* 'people' (2); *ikona* 'picture' (2); *simpan* 'universe' (6); *gnorizo* 'know' (3); *iparkho* 'exist' (6); *khronos* 'time' (5); *arkhi* 'beginning' (2); *apandisi* 'answers' (2); *yi* 'earth' (3); *evnoitos* 'obvious' (2); *anoitos* 'silly' (2); *stirizo* 'supported' (2); *apiri sira apo trapulo kharta* 'infinite series of cards' (2).
	When faced with lexical gaps, a translator is forced to replace a SL item with a different TL item, such as using a more general word to translate a more specific word. In so doing, the collocational chain in the original text may be compromised. In this case, the translator must ensure that the TT holds together lexically in its own way.	In an English text advertising carpets, the following words create a kind of collocational chain: 'plant' (rather than 'factory'), 'qualities' (rather than 'kinds' or 'types'), 'complementary colours' (rather than 'matching colours'), 'select' (rather than 'choose'), and 'discerning'. Arabic is unable to distinguish between 'plant' and 'factory', and between 'select' and 'choose', and has no direct equivalent for 'complementary' and 'discerning'. In the Arabic translation, 'complementary' is paraphrased as 'the colours of which match the rest of the colours of the collection' and 'discerning' is dropped. All of this changes the collocational patterning of the ST, replacing it with one that is more reiterative.

Try this

The following tagline appears on a napkin distributed onboard a Delta Airlines flight:

SPILL YOUR DRINK. OR YOUR THOUGHTS.
That's What These Are Here For.

With reference to the concept of lexical cohesion, translate this into any language of your choice and justify your translation. Consider the following:

1. The tagline is clearly playing with the word 'spill'. The technical word for this rhetorical device is **zeugma**. In your chosen TL, how would you reproduce the cohesive link between 'spill your drink' and 'spill your thought'? Remember that you don't necessarily have to use the word 'spill' in the TL, but the same cohesive pattern should preferably be used.

2. Also keep in mind that this tagline is on a napkin, a nonverbal modality that creates cohesion with the word 'spill'. So how would you further create cohesion between your textual translation and the napkin as a material entity?

Under felicitous circumstances, it might be possible to preserve visual-verbal cohesion with the direct transfer of words. An example is from the London-based food chain Pret A Manger. In its Hong Kong branches, Pret displays bilingual posters in its shops. In one of these posters is written the tagline SUPER-NATURAL. The visual component of the poster shows an image of a 'phantom' (a cute one) that constitutes a cabbage leaf as its blanket-head and two limes as its eyes.

This is another excellent instance of multimodal communication, where the verbal text interacts with the visual text to produce meaning. This text-image interplay generates two readings from the tagline: 'supernatural' (as in out of the ordinary), and 'super natural' (as in extremely natural). This bifurcated reading is encouraged by a typographical detail, where a hyphen separates the two morphemes in the tagline.

To English-language readers, the double entendre is obvious. On the one hand, the primary point being made is that Pret uses natural ingredients (pointing to the vegetables that make up the 'ghost' in the visual), hence 'super (extremely) natural'; on the other hand, supernatural (ghostly) as a single word-concept is very common in English and creates paradoxical humour when read against the phantom image in the poster. The contradictory senses of 'very natural' and 'not natural' are ingeniously collapsed into a text-image combo.

The accompanying Chinese tagline, unfortunately, misses the point. It says: 'pure and natural' (back-translated). This translates one of the two layers of signification in the original, and disrupts the intersemiotic link between the text and the image. After all, purity and naturalness has nothing to do with the sense of ghostliness; consequently, the humour is lost in translation. Using the terms of art of Hallidayan linguistics, we will say that the word-image cohesion between the caption and the image is compromised in the translation.

The obvious solution, which in this case happens to be a morphemic translation, is *chao·ziran*, corresponding exactly to SUPER-NATURAL, except that the hyphen would be changed to a middle dot in accordance with Chinese conventions. As with the English tagline, this can be interpreted in Chinese as 'extremely natural' (an abridgement of *chaoji ziran*); it can also be treated as a single word denoting the ghostly realm, literally 'beyond the natural'. This proposed translation allows the Chinese reader to appreciate the double-layeredness of the key word, and would elicit the same response (which could be a laugh) from the reader (recall the idea of dynamic equivalence from Chapter 2). More to the point of what we are saying in this chapter, it also preserves the intersemiotic cohesive relation between text and image in the ST.

Another bilingual poster, also by Pret, features the tagline TRICKY INGREDIENTS. This example is relevant to lexical cohesion in that it plays with an unusual and ambiguous collocation, from where the rhetorical force of the tagline is derived. It is not immediately clear what 'tricky' means in this context, but the main text does give us some hints: 'We love using tricky stuff like fresh avocado, very crispy bacon and fresh salad leaves.'

But in what specific sense are these items 'tricky'? It could be that they are so fresh and crispy that their shelf-life is limited, which makes them very delicate to deal with, hence the 'trickiness'. Or has it also to do with the image, which shows an odd combination of vegetables: a messy bundle of sprouts on an onion, resembling uncombed hair on someone's head. (Or is this all my imagination? I hope we're getting at the whole idea of trickiness now – this poster makes us pause and ponder.)

The given Chinese translation, however, does not sound so tricky; it reads: 'Exquisite Ingredients.' This might convey the idea of freshness and delicacy, but rhetorically speaking it is unexceptional, for the

Try this

With reference to the two Pret posters discussed above, how would you translate SUPER-NATURAL and TRICKY INGREDIENTS into a TL of your choice? Remember that your translated tagline must retain the proposition in the ST (naturalness/freshness of ingredients) and also cohere with the visuals of the respective posters.

collocation is unmarked and therefore mundane-sounding in Chinese. To convey the markedness of the tagline in the SL, one needs to find an equally marked construction in the TL, which simultaneously captures the central message, that is, the absolute freshness of the ingredients.

A possible candidate for the translation could be the hyperbolic slang word for 'fresh' in Hong Kong-style Chinese: *sin'baau*, literally 'fresh to the point of bursting'. Combined with the word for ingredients in Chinese, this would mean 'extremely fresh ingredients', but in a way that is slightly irreverent and fun. The idea of bursting also coheres with the image, where the sprouts look very much exploded all over the onion.

Last but not least is **coherence**, which belongs to the realm of pragmatics. Unlike cohesion, coherence refers to the conceptual, as opposed to textual-linguistic, network that binds different elements of a text together. For example, if a text mentions 'Hillary Clinton' in the first instance and subsequently mentions 'the ex-First Lady' and 'the former New York Senator', we know that the latter two phrases refer back to Clinton, but this knowledge is premised on our knowledge of American politics. In other words, the links among 'Clinton', 'First Lady', and 'New York Senator' are not built into the text linguistically.

In translation, one must not take such extra-textual knowledge for granted: what is presupposed as common or general knowledge to the ST reader may or may not be the same for the prospective TT reader. In an example from Baker (2011: 232), a text mentions 'Harrods' in one paragraph; in the following paragraph, Harrods is being referred to with the phrase 'the splendid Knightsbridge store'. To the British reader or indeed anyone who is aware of Harrods, there is coherence between the precedent word on the one hand and the subsequent phrase on the other, based on the knowledge that the famous Harrods shop is located at Knightsbridge in London. The Arabic translation applies the procedure of explicitation: it stretches 'Harrods' into 'the main store Harrods'; doing so allows the word 'store' to lexically cohere with the word 'store' in 'the splendid Knightsbridge store', which is retained in the Arabic translation, hence allowing the Arabic reader to connect the two.

Discourse considerations supplement the intra-sentential perspective of the equivalence paradigm. They are instructive, given that translators always work with entire texts, not individual sentences. Even if you are commissioned to translate a single tagline, the discourse consideration of verbal-nonverbal cohesion comes into play. A comparative discourse perspective thus allows us to consider translational issues on a higher plane of linguistic analysis. Mona Baker sums this up succinctly for us:

> Every language has its own battery of devices for creating links between textual elements. Unless the translator is carrying out some kind of linguistic exercise, for instance for research purposes, transferring the devices used in the source text into the target text will not do. Under normal circumstances, what is required is a reworking of the methods of establishing links to suit the textual norms of the target language. The grammatical system of each language will itself encourage the use of certain devices in preference to others. The textual norms of each genre will further suggest certain options and rule out others that are grammatically acceptable and may, in other genres, be textually acceptable as well.
>
> (Baker 2011: 198)

Register analysis: Hatim and Mason's model

The term register, on a most basic level, refers to the level of formality at which a piece of discourse is pegged. As a matter of principle, a translator should ensure that the register of the ST is not compromised in the TT, as in rendering a formal text in an informal manner, or vice versa. The exception is, of course, when such register shift is intended by the skopos of the translation commission (e.g., when adapting a novel for young readers or a scientific text for lay readers). At any rate all of this entails the selection of appropriate words and structures in alignment with the register desired in the circumstances.

A simple illustration: in Japanese both *oishii* and *umai* mean 'delicious', with the latter being more casual than the former. In one scene from a Japanese movie, a crude and broken man was sitting among several elderly ladies, eating the food they had cooked for him; as he was eating he murmured the word *umai* repeatedly. The choice of *umai* over *oishii* is strategic in this setting. If we were to subtitle *umai* as 'delicious' we would be missing the intended register, though it would not count as a mistranslation. So which English word can we use here? 'Tasty' is hardly a better choice, for it is about equivalent to 'delicious' in terms of register; 'delectable' would be plainly wrong, for it sounds more learned (and therefore is of a higher register) than 'delicious'.

If you check up a thesaurus, 'yummy' might come across as the closest equivalent to *umai* in terms of register; but 'yummy' sounds a tad too cute to be uttered by the crude man in the scene. The subtitler goes for a brilliant yet deceptively simple option: *Mmm*. Here an interjection, essentially a sound, expressing contentment in English aptly translates the Japanese word, conveying not primarily the semantics of *umai*, but the casual and spontaneous emotion emanating from it.

Different languages have different register divisions; and the distinction is sometimes not simply between the formal and the informal, or between written and spoken varieties. Some languages are more nuanced than others when it comes to codifying social hierarchy in language. We have already seen, for example, that some Asian languages are highly sensitive to factors such as the proximity of relationship between interlocutors and their relative social status and/or age. It is a trite rule that a translator should translate into a TL register that is in accord with the expectations of its native users. In considering such factors we are in the realm of **sociolinguistics**, which is especially pertinent to the discourse paradigm in translation studies.

In Thai, for example, an entire register called the *racha sap* is reserved for communications with, as well as in relation to, a member of the royal family (and this is already a simplified picture: there are several tiers within the royal hierarchy each of which has a different register associated with it). In Thai media discourse, when describing the activities of a royal person, a completely different lexicon needs to be invoked. For example, the verb 'go' in ordinary Thai is *pai*, but when used with reference to royalty (e.g., 'the Crown Princess went to ...'), it becomes the much longer *sadet phra ratchadamnoen*.

Indeed the difference between the ordinary and royal registers is so distinct in Thai that there exist specialised manuals to guide speakers on the proper use of this privileged lexicon in the event that they need it. An ordinary Thai person on the street would seldom, if ever at all, have the opportunity to actually use this register (though educated persons would have at least a listening proficiency in it). But officials or other persons who need to interact with royal dignitaries in the course of their duty are obliged to *convert* their ordinary language into *royal-speak* when communicating with or referring to a royal member. In so doing they are performing an act of intralingual translation (see p.72). In fact, the *racha sap* is also incorporated into the Thai school curriculum, where students learn how words (nouns, verbs, pronouns, discourse particles, etc.) morph into different forms when they occur in the royal register.

In its more technical sense, register is a central concept in SFL. Basil Hatim and Ian Mason, who also draw upon Hallidayan linguistics, have developed a register-based model for translation analysis in their books *Discourse and the Translator* (1990) and *The Translator as Communicator* (1997). Register in SFL has a tripartite structure comprising **Field**, **Tenor**, and **Mode**. Table 4.8 explains these constituents of register.

Try this

In addition to *royal-speak*, there is also what we may call *monk-speak* in Thai. This entails yet another set of vocabulary, comprising words and phrases expressing reverence, used when speaking with monks. There is additionally the *phasa phra* ('monk language'), which includes a set of lexicon used to describe monks' activities and also characterises the style of writing in Buddhist-related texts.

Such linguistic phenomenon is peculiar to deeply religious societies such as Thailand, where ordained monks are highly revered, and points to how language encapsulates and responds to cultural realities. The lesson for the translator is first to appreciate that language is contingent on the sociolinguistics of the culture in which it is embedded, and second to become sensitised to it, especially where the ST involves references to specific persons (in this case, monks) that may trigger the use of a different register.

Can you find a comparable or analogous linguistic phenomenon in your own culture or in another culture with which you are familiar?

Table 4.8 Register analysis

Concept	Components	Functional Description	Linguistic (Lexicogrammatical) Manifestation	Explanation
Register	**Field**: subject matter (e.g., legal advice to client; press release by corporate company; sports commentary)	**Ideational function** – the conveyance of information, ideas, and experience through the text	• Subject-specific terms • Transitivity: choice of voice (active/ passive); nominalisation (non-noun forms→noun forms); use of different verbal structures to indicate different processes, etc.	'Language users generate **ideational** meanings which are ultimately realized in the actual choices made within linguistic systems such as those of **transitivity** (the way we view reality and represent it in the arrangement of the clause in terms of participants, processes and circumstances)' (Hatim & Mason 1997: 19).
	Tenor: level of formality (e.g., highly formal; journalistic style; colloquialism, bureaucratese)	**Interpersonal function** – the relationship between text-producer and text-receiver as established in the text	• Proximity: pronouns (first/second/ third person; inclusive/exclusive) index varying degrees of closeness with text-receiver • Mood: sentence forms indicate whether an utterance is a statement, question, or order/request • Modality: modal verbs express varying degrees of certainty with respect to the proposition of the utterance • Stance: evaluative attitude of the speaker or writer	'Choices made within the **interpersonal** function of language, and finds expression in the **mood** and **modality** in actual texts. Mood covers the three basic sentence forms: the declarative, the interrogative and the imperative. Modality reflects the attitude towards the status of what is expressed' (Hatim & Mason 1997: 19).
	Mode: written, spoken, or multimodal (e.g., a piece of written legislation vs. electoral debates vs. TV advertisement)	**Textual function** – how a well-formed piece of discourse is being produced	Thematic and information structures; cohesion (see previous section on Baker's model)	'Mode (which we characterized … in terms of the physical distance between producer and receiver, and between producer and object description) also motivates various procedures undertaken within the so-called **textual** function of language' (Hatim & Mason 1997: 20).

Germane to translation analysis is the **static-dynamic continuum model** advanced by Hatim and Mason (1997). This model postulates that in communication, we straddle between two endpoints. On the one pole, there is communicative behaviour that is *expectation-fulfilling* and *norm-confirming*; here interaction is 'static', achieves *maximal stability*, and generates stylistically unmarked texts. On the other pole, there is communicative behaviour that is *expectation-defying* and *norm-flouting*; in this case, interaction is 'dynamic' or *turbulent*, achieves *minimal stability*, and generates stylistically marked texts. Where we place a communicative event along this spectrum would depend on the specific linguistic performance that occurs. Suppose I were a barrister fighting a case for my client. In the courtroom, I will manage my linguistic performance in line with the discursive norms of the legal profession and expectations of the general public. Using register analysis, I might prescribe the following guidelines for myself:

1. **Field:** Use appropriate terms of art in law (e.g., in legal discourse, the 'denial' of an allegation and the 'non-admission' of an allegation are not the same thing); invoke relevant primary legislation ('Under section 10(1) of the Counter-Terrorism and Security Act 2015'); and cite precedent case law from authoritative sources to support my arguments ('I refer the Court to the case of *Dursan v. J. Sainsbury PLC*, reported in …'). Use active constructions to foreground agency and passive constructions to suppress agency where this is deemed to be advantageous for my client's case (*transitivity*).
2. **Tenor:** Use formal verbal structures in the appropriate *mood* – declarative for material facts, interrogative in cross-examination, imperative when beseeching the jury's empathy. Use appropriate modal verbs to express the desired degree of certainty (*modality*). Use pronouns strategically, for example, the third person pronoun to project a detached tone; the inclusive 'we' to create proximity with other participants in the litigation.
3. **Mode:** Speak clearly, cohesively, and coherently; supplement this with a rich repertoire of body language when asserting a point.

If I were to adhere to the above guidelines closely, I would be enacting an instance of static and stable communication; but if I were to flout all the guidelines (speak in the vernacular, use non-legal vocabulary without citation, employ loose sentence structures, exhibit erratic body language, etc.), I would be destabilising the norms and introducing turbulence into courtroom discourse; and if I were to conform to some of

Try this

In the landmark English Court of Appeal case *Ladd v. Marshall* [1954] 3 All ER 745, Lord Denning famously set down the guidelines on the admissibility of new evidence in appeal cases. The following is an oft-cited passage (the punctuation scheme is as in the original):

> It is very rare that application is made to this court for a new trial on the ground that a witness has told a lie. The principles to be applied are the same as those always applied when fresh evidence is sought to be introduced. In order to justify the reception of fresh evidence or a new trial, three conditions must be fulfilled: first, it must be shown that the evidence could not have been obtained with reasonable diligence for use at the trial: second, the evidence must be such that, if given, it would probably have an important influence on the result of the case, although it need not be decisive: thirdly, the evidence must be such as is presumably to be believed, or in other words, it must be apparently credible, although it need not be incontrovertible. (748)

With reference to the various aspects of register discussed above, translate (or interpret, imagining a court scenario) the above passage into a TL of your choice. How would you evaluate your own translation (or interpreting) based on Hatim and Mason's static-dynamic continuum model?

the norms but contravene others, my linguistic performance would be positioned at some point between the static-dynamic continuum.

The relevance of all this for translating may be encapsulated as follows: if a ST at some point exhibits a motivated instance of dynamic communication, the TT should be similarly marked at the corresponding point. This can be illustrated with an example from Judy Wakayabashi's study of the Japanese script in translation. In Haruki Murakami's popular novel *1Q84*, there is a dyslexic character whose speech is represented using a mixture of *hiragana* and *katakana* (two types of Japanese script, the first used mainly to represent grammatical words and the latter to transliterate foreign words), as opposed to using kanji – Sino-Japanese characters used to represent most content words in Japanese writing. In so doing, the novelist introduces a dynamic element into the written discourse to distinguish the dyslexic utterance from ordinary, unmarked utterances.

For example, in one instance the words 'capitalism' and 'materialism', which would normally be represented in kanji, are cast instead in kata-kana when uttered by the dyslexic character. This is the aspect of Mode in register analysis – the way in which the words are written contravenes normative practice, defies expectations, and generates rupture in linear reading. This enables readers to appreciate that there is something amiss in the way the character speaks in the novel's constructed world.

How do we manage this linguistic turbulence when translating the same utterance into another language? This certainly calls for creativity, and there have been some successful attempts. The Polish translator uses lower-case for the utterance throughout, including at the start of the sentence. The Swedish translator breaks up each word into separate syllables using hyphenation, indexing the monotony of the character's diction. A similar strategy is used in the English translation, where 'capitalism' becomes 'cap-i-tal-izum' and 'materialism' becomes 'ma-teer-ee-al-izum' (Wakayabashi 2016: 180).

Using register analysis in respect of the English translation, we would first state that the atypical form of script in the Japanese original – the Mode of the discourse – is motivated by the need to visually represent dyslexic speech patterns. The English translation uses two techniques to render the visual dynamic in the ST into an aural dynamic in the TT: first, the words are segmented and hyphenated to recreate a sense of reading impediment; second, the spelling is deliberately corrupted to mimic imperfect enunciation. Using resources in the TL, the translator innovates aberrant spacing and spelling to signal strenuous diction. In so doing, the translator responds to the register shift in the ST (realised through slippage between visual scripts) with the idea of non-normativity in speech (realised through auditory nuances) in the TT.

If, however, a certain linguistic choice delivers static communication in the ST, which means to say it is norm-conforming and expectation-fulfilling, it should in principle remain so in the TT. An example would be the use of pronouns, belonging to the domain of Tenor, in academic discourse. Contemporary English writers, at least in the humanities field, frequently use the first-person singular pronoun in subject position when expressing stance ('I would argue that ...'; 'I disagree with ...'). This norm is far from universal. Chinese academics generally prefer an impersonal noun ('this essay argues that ...') instead of a pronoun in subject position; where pronouns are used, the preference is for the first-person plural even if the referent is singular, that is, a single author may refer to himself or herself as 'we'. The first-person singular pronoun, if used extensively, comes across as intrusive and egotistical, and constitutes a marked choice in Chinese academic writing.

Therefore, when translating an English academic treatise into Chinese, if one observes a recurrence of first-person pronouns in subject position, it might be possible to turn at least some of those pronouns in the English into generic nouns or first-person plural pronouns in the Chinese, or even to drop them through syntactic restructuring. Along similar lines, Olohan (2016: 164–165), citing Perales-Escudero and Swales (2011), reports that when English academic abstracts are translated into Spanish, there is evidence of enhanced boosting ('one of the most significant results'), reduced hedging ('to our knowledge'), and increased attitudinal marking ('seems surprising') in the TT. These shifts in effect adapt the register of Anglophone discourse to Hispanic conventions.

So it seems that where there is a discrepancy between two languages in respect of register, the translator should fine-tune the discursive constitution of the ST. However, it is possible to argue to the contrary with recourse to text-type theory (see Chapter 3): an academic treatise is partially an expressive text, which requires that the form of the ST be retained. Pronominal choice is a formal consideration. For example, in the case of an authoritative work by a renowned scholar, where first-person pronouns have the function of establishing the writer's academic authority, these pronouns should probably be retained in translation, even if doing so runs counter to TL discourse conventions. This illustrates how textual considerations coming from different paradigms may conflict with each other and must be resolved with regard to the contingent circumstances of the communicative event.

Here is an authentic example of how translation negotiates the register of academic texts, reported by Bennett (2013: 174–176). Extract 1 is a Portuguese history article translated literally into English, while Extract 2 is the actual English translation (my emphases).

Extract 1 (Literal translation of a Portuguese history article)
Starting from the premise that, in the Early Modern period, access to certain goods and services indicated the social, material and cultural distance of individuals and knowing that, from early on, the different kingdoms were concerned to create obstacles to the consumption of luxury goods, through legislation,

accentuating the differences between social groups and understanding that luxury damaged the good order of the kingdom due to the exit of money, **we cannot fail to note** that the possession of realty and chattels indicated the place of each one in society. **Thus thought the theoreticians** of the economy and social order and **thus thought the moralists**, only **starting to be manifested dissonant voices** during the eighteenth century.

Extract 2 (Final English translation)
In the Early Modern period, the social, material and cultural position of individuals could be judged by the access that they had to certain goods and services. **However**, from early on, many kingdoms tried to block the consumption of luxury goods through legislation on the grounds that such items drained the financial resources of the country, leading to disarray (**a belief that was held** by both **theoreticians** of the social/economic order and by **moralists**, and which persisted through to the eighteenth century, when **dissenting voices started to be heard**). This legislation accentuated the differences between social groups, with the result that the ownership of property, both realty and chattels, offered a reliable indication of an individual's status in society.

Comparing the two texts, what stands out in relief is how the English translation has reshaped the narrative of the Portuguese original by altering its discourse pattern. The TT imposes a chronological and logical structure (the addition of 'However') on the ST, which uses instead an embedded and circumlocutory pattern (the winding sentence that begins 'Starting from the premise that …'). The TT also mitigates the interpersonal tone of the ST ('we cannot fail to note') and its rhetorical flourishes (e.g., parallelism in 'Thus thought the … Thus thought the …'; inversion in 'starting to be manifested dissonant voices', cf. 'dissenting voices started to be heard'). Overall, the register of the English translation is characterised by a highly instrumentalist Tenor, a quality that emerges through its linguistic choices and thematic structure; this departs from the more lyrical and indirect mode of narration that constitutes the unique register of the Portuguese original.

Imagine you were asked to translate a Portuguese academic article for publication in an English-language periodical. Register would be one of the obstacles standing in your way. Bennett (2007: 157) holds that English academic discourse generally projects an ideology of positivism and empiricism toward knowledge production. This is textualised through lexicogrammatical (words and structures) means, including the use of nominalisations and passive constructions, which suppress agency and emanate a sense of scientific detachment. Following our Register model, these come under 'transitivity', which instantiates the Field of discourse. In terms of lexis, English academic discourse prefers 'matter-of-fact' words as opposed to 'flamboyant emotive terms' (157); the latter kind of vocabulary are integral to the Portuguese discursive tradition. This difference is one of Tenor.

From a prescriptive-applied angle, we would posit that a translator needs to take into account these differences in register inherent in the two academic traditions, and where necessary change the discourse pattern of the Portuguese text to accommodate the conventions of English. This is a pragmatic and practical standpoint: after all, the purpose of translating a Portuguese scholarly article for publication in an English-language journal is for it to gain visibility in international academia. It might therefore seem perfectly legitimate for the translator to adapt the ST to suit the register conventions of the host language and culture.

However, if we come from a descriptive-conceptual perspective, as does Bennett, we would come to a very different conclusion, namely that the imposition of a discourse structure familiar to Anglophone readers on a Portuguese text is an act of virtual violence. This kind of discursive violence is termed **epistemicide**, and is seen as an undesirable trait that should be 'combated' (Bennett 2013), because it exacerbates unequal power relations between hegemonic and less dominant languages.

This has implications for practice and pedagogy. Bennett (2013) suggests ways in which we can train translation students to resist succumbing to Anglophone discourse through critical analysis of varied discursive traditions; learning to write in the style of Anglophone scholarly discourse so as to subvert it; and developing strategies to mediate and negotiate with stakeholders in academia. This position is in line with Perales-Escudero and Swales' (2011: 67) recommendation for academic translators working from English to preserve rhetorical patterns unique to the TL, rather than import common English usage.

Bennett is well aware of the practical issues in combating epistemicide: translated articles may be turned down by international forums on the grounds that they detract from the discourse orientations of Anglophone writing. On this point, Bennett (2013) emphasises the need for translators to 'exercise agency by responding to reviewers' comments or by writing publishable letters to the editor to explain the issues involved' (188), and suggests that such mediation skills be part of a translator training programme:

> [Translators] need to be able to explain such issues to the various parties involved in the process. Authors, for example, need to understand just why aspects of their discourse are problematic to translate, while text receivers (journal editors, conference organizers) need to know the reasons for less conventional translation choices. When these result from cultural gaps on the lexical or grammatical levels, translators have traditionally resorted to notes or prefaces to clarify the issue. However, the issue is much more complex when the entire discourse is oriented differently ... In this situation, a more in-depth explanation may be needed that draws upon a broad historical and cultural (as well as linguistic) knowledge base. Translators can thus be trained to present such arguments for the benefit of the various stakeholders involved.
>
> (Bennett 2013: 187)

Measuring translation quality: House's model

We close this chapter with Juliane House's Translation Quality Assessment (TQA) model, first proposed in 1977 and revised in 2015. The assessment of translation quality lies at the core of the prescriptive enterprise. After all, to prescribe translation methods is to: (1) gain access to samples of translating work; (2) appraise what they did right as well as what they did wrong; and (3) devise principles or rules to guide future practice.

As with Baker and also Hatim and Mason, House (2015) bases her model on SFL, specifically on the triadic notions of Field, Tenor, and Mode that together make up the register of a text. For this, Table 4.8 above still works for us, though House has slightly different specifications for each category. Her model is divided into several stages, which I reformulate into a set of procedural operations as follows:

Stage 1: *Generate the ST register profile*
This means to analyse the ST according to the dimensions of Field, Tenor, and Mode, a process that involves eliciting the 'linguistic correlates' of each category. For example, if the passive voice is a recursive feature of a text,

then that would come under Field; if a text uses emotive lexicon or colloquial expressions where 'neutral' options are available, that would be a feature under Tenor; and if a text is hung together through the repetition of a number of keywords, we will note that down under Mode. Remember that the purpose of this stage is not to get ourselves totally lost in the labyrinth of terminology. Rather, at the end of this preliminary analysis, we should be able to come up with a general formulation about the ST register.

Stage 2: *Identify the genre of the ST as generated by its register*

The term **genre** is a SFL concept that refers to a conventionalised text category associated with a particular communicative function. For example, a CEO's message on the website of a multinational company belongs to the genre of corporate communication. The distinction between text type (Chapter 3) and genre can be amorphous, but generally speaking a single text type or text function (informative, expressive, operative) can be realised by various different genres. For example, a financial report distributed to shareholders and a feature article in a newsletter are two different genres by virtue of their being conventionalised in different communicative environments, even though both are functionally informative.

Stage 3: *Produce a 'statement of function' for the ST*

This basically summarises what the ST is about (the ideational function), what kind of relationship is constructed between the text-producer and text-receiver (the interpersonal function), and also how the discourse is built up (the textual function).

Stage 4: *Repeat Stages 1–3 for the TT*

Stage 5: *Error identification*

Compare the ST and TT register profiles and identify 'mismatches' or 'errors' (note how the choice of words here shows the highly prescriptive nature of TQA). These include 'dimensional' and 'non-dimensional errors'. **Dimensional errors** occur when the TT shifts away from the ST in terms of its register or generic features; **non-dimensional errors** include denotative errors (the ST is misrepresented at particular points) and target-system errors (the TT fails to conform to linguistic norms in the TL).

Stage 6: *Make a 'statement of quality' of the TT*

This encapsulates our assessment and evaluation of the overall quality of the translation.

The strength of the TQA framework lies in its very neat structure; however, its actual application may or may not eventually generate a satisfactory statement of quality. This is mainly because the mismatches between the ST and the TT are not always errors in the sense of erroneous mistakes: while the so-called non-dimensional errors pertaining to meaning and TL norms may be seen as erroneous, dimensional errors relating to register and genre may in fact be intentional pragmatic shifts and should not be subject to a simplistic criticism without further scrutiny of the underlying motives. House's own application of the model on an English corporate annual report and its German translation (House 2015: 127–143) fails to derive a conclusive assessment of the TT. There is also quite a bit of overlap and redundancy in her analysis of Field, Tenor, and Mode for the ST and the TT, which is contrary to the structural neatness of the model.

In the following paragraphs, I model on and at the same time stream-line House's application of her TQA model to analyse another text of the same genre. This is a bilingual annual report of InspiringHK Sports Foundation (2016: 7, 51), a Hong Kong-based non-governmental organisation. We look specifically at a preface by the foundation's Chief Campaigner; the SL is Chinese and the TL English. In this analysis, I have fine-tuned House's analytical framework set out above, but have adhered to her general method of comparing ST and TT in respect of their register.

Case analysis of Chief Campaigner's speech in InspiringHK Sports Foundation annual report

Field

In terms of its Field, the text at hand is a message from the management of InspiringHK Sports Foundation to its stakeholders, including prospective donors. It is a kind of mission statement that establishes the shared values and corporate identity of the organisation. This function is lexicogrammatically realised in the ST, where words with very positive connotations are used to talk about the various activities rolled out by the foundation in the service of the community at large. The English translation tones down the optimistic vibes of the ST, using instead expressions that are rhetorically neutral.

For example, whereas the ST says 'giving earnest and enthusiastic [renzhen jiji] students the opportunity to continuously [chixu] receive training in sports', the TT says 'giving more youth the opportunity to take part in sports programmes'. Here we move from students *receiving training* (ST) to students *taking part in sports programmes* (TT), where the former brings forth the status of the students as beneficiaries much more clearly than the latter, and the recasting of 'training' into 'programmes' arguably adds a corporate flavour to the English translation. The omission of *renzhen jiji* ('earnest and enthusiastic') and *chixu* ('continuously') also gives the translation a more matter-of-fact tone.

The English TT cuts down on lexical redundancies in the Chinese text considerably: *zhuanye guanzhi* ('professional governance') becomes simply 'governance'; *momo gongxian* ('silently contributed') is reduced to 'contributed'; *zhangmu qingxi ji touming* ('accounts [are] clear and transparent') becomes 'our finances are transparent'. It also reconstructs and demetaphorises some of the Chinese expressions. For example, one sentence in the English translation reads: 'They worked into nights and contributed their valuable resources … to advance the foundation.' In the original Chinese, two lexicalised metaphors are deployed, namely *shengeng xizuo*, literally 'deep ploughing and intense cultivation' (*Oxford Chinese Dictionary*), corresponding to 'worked into nights' in the English; and *daqiao pulu*, literally 'build bridges and lay roads', translated as 'advance [the foundation]'. The figurative language of the Chinese text evokes the image of an impassioned charity foundation closely engaged with society; the translation however is much more literal and direct, conjuring up the image of a commercial company conducting a charitable business.

There are a number of substantial omissions in the translation; these are mostly 'soft' expressions that do not convey material facts. The following Chinese sentences, rendered closely in English below, do not appear in the translation:

If the student members of InspiringHK are our most precious assets, then every destined person who supports us by advancing the development of InspiringHK and mobilising all sectors of society are our most treasured resources. (my translation)

The expression 'destined person' (*youyuan ren*, literally people with whom we have a predestined connection) is culture-specific, evoking Chinese metaphysical notions of fate and providence. This sentence expresses the foundation's gratitude to its donors, using stylised phrases like 'most precious assets' (*zui zhenxi de zichan*) and 'most treasured resources' (*zui baogui de ziyuan*), which would sound melodramatic if literally translated into the English version. Other similar truncations are observable, for example:

> It is exactly because of everyone's selfless efforts in the year 2015-16 that we have the honour of winning the 6th Hong Kong Volunteer Awards. Here, we thank all of you for your support from the bottom of our hearts, and promise we'll do a better job in the coming year! (my translation)

In the English translation, this becomes simply: 'This is evidenced by us winning accolades in the 6th Hong Kong Volunteer Awards.' Notice, besides the obvious omission, that the last Chinese sentence is exclamatory, whereas the English translation is a straightforward, no-frills declarative statement. Once again we see the translator's inclination to mitigate the expressive, even celebratory, mood of the ST by omitting repetitive expressions of gratitude and boiling the discourse down to the material facts.

Overall, the linguistic choices in the TT have the combined effect of reconstructing the contribution of the charity foundation to Hong Kong society as a matter of corporate importance rather than a purely philanthropic act.

Tenor

In terms of Tenor, the English translation uses more first-person exclusive pronouns in the plural than the Chinese original. For example, the Chinese original has a line that goes like this:

> There are victories and losses in competitions, but the most important thing is that *they* are given the opportunity to improve self-confidence, develop sportsmanship and learn to set goals in life through these competitions. (my translation and emphasis)

This translates into English as:

> They may win or lose, but most importantly *we want them to* improve self-confidence, develop sportsmanship and learn to set goals in life. (emphasis added)

The added 'we' in the TT turns the perspective around and imbues the foundation rather than the sports participants (the beneficiaries of the charity scheme) with agency. This stance is in accord with the corporate tone of the English version.

The grammatical constructions in the translation tend to be more direct: whereas the Chinese original says, '*The core function of the InspiringHK Sports Foundation is to provide ...*', the translation says, 'InspiringHK Sports Foundation provides ...' Also, for the Chinese clause 'We owe all the achievements of InspiringHK to a group of hardworking Volunteer Board of Directors, Volunteer Executives and Full Time Executives', the English translation says, 'Throughout the year our Volunteer Board of Directors, Volunteer Executives and Full Time Executives made it all happen through sweat and toil.' Based on the last example, we might say that the interpersonal element in the English translation is weaker than that in the original Chinese. Although the TT features more first-person plural pronouns than the ST, these tend to be exclusive rather than inclusive pronouns, and they go some way toward grounding the corporate identity of the foundation rather than fostering rapport with readers and stakeholders. This difference in interpersonal function is best exemplified by the following example:

ST: In addition, *we have successfully* matched 42 mentees with their mentors through our Mentorship Programme, *giving them a brother or sister to share their pleasures and pains in the course of their growing up.* (my translation and emphasis)

TT: Our Mentorship Programme has seen the matching of 42 mentors and mentees, who get a person who they can share with.

Clearly, while the two texts relay the same core information, that is, the Mentorship Programme, the ST is more interested in flourishing its discourse with heart-warming rhetoric evoking quasi-kinship ties: 'giving them a brother or sister [*gege jiejie*] to share their pleasures and pains in the course of their growing up', where the informal *gege jiejie* invokes a familial, almost childlike, ambience, as opposed to the slightly more formal *xiongdi jiemei*, which also means brothers and sisters. The TT, by contrast, sets aside this emotive verbiage and goes straight to the point ('get a person who they can share with').

Mode

In terms of Mode, the original Chinese sounds more like a speech than a formally written text. Its discourse is more cohesive and also more circular than the English translation, in large part thanks to its repetitive, recursive style. Notably there is a plethora of appellative expressions in the ST that convey the Chief Campaigner's gratitude to the various supporters of the foundation; as we have seen, some of these are deleted or truncated in the English translation. For example:

> ST: We are *also* pleased to collaborate with more charity organisations and schools to recruit students and provide experiential learning activities, to enable InspiringHK's culture of giving [*juanxian wenhua*] to cover four aspects, including: *giving* money, *giving* time, *giving* knowledge and skills, and *giving* social networks. Everyone can contribute to charity through InspiringHK. (my translation and emphasis)

> TT: The enabler of all this is InspiringHK's giving culture, which covers the giving of time, skills, network and money.

Apart from the obvious omission, the incessant repetition of *juanxian* ('giving' or 'donating') in the ST is cut down considerably in the TT, which fulfils the linguistic norms of English. Although both texts belong to the written register, the discourse of the TT is much less elaborate, and therefore sounds less spontaneous than the original. In the following examples, entire clauses in the Chinese original are being cut out:

> ST: *In terms of expenditure*, over 80% of expenses were spent *directly* on sports programmes, *[we] ensure that donations are used in the right places*, [so as to] make a real impact on society. (my translation and emphasis)

> TT: 80% of expenses were spent on sports programmes to make a real impact on society.

> ST: [We have] presented the organisation's service philosophy through major mass media in Hong Kong in more than 20 interviews *and through social media, to let the public know more about the sports charity platform of InspiringHK.* (my translation and emphasis)

> TT: Media outlets in Hong Kong reported us more than 20 times, for which we are very grateful.

In these examples, the translator condenses the Chinese original, removing whole clauses that would have made the English text unnaturally reiterative. The resultant translation is skeletal and streamlined compared to the more richly textured ST.

Genre

Now we come to genre specification. For this we turn to the title of the text and also of the publication in which it is embedded. The Chinese text is titled *zong ganshi de hua*, or 'Chief Campaigner's words'; compare this to the title of the English translation, 'Chief Campaigner's report'. Whereas the ST positions itself as a piece of verbal communication, the English translation stands more like a corporate document. This point is corroborated by the title of the whole publication: 'Annual Report' (*zhounian baogao*) in Chinese versus 'Impact Report' in English. The latter has a strong corporate overtone that underpins the register and overall function of the translation.

Statement of function

And what is this overall function; in other words, what is our 'statement of function' for the ST and the TT? Our preceding analysis indicates that the register of the translation has the following features vis-à-vis the original Chinese text: it is more detached, that is, less emotionally involved (ideational function); it foregrounds the corporate identity of the foundation more than it seeks to establish rapport with readers (interpersonal function); and it is a more direct, less elaborate piece of discourse without unnecessary repetition (textual function).

Error identification

In terms of what are called non-dimensional errors, there are almost no denotative errors (except at one point where '*over* 80% of expenses' is translated as '80% of expenses'); the translation fully conforms with the linguistic norms of the English language, and so there are no target-system errors either. But there are several omissions, as we have observed. Are these considered errors? There are also the dimensional errors: the TT has moved away from the ST significantly in terms of register and genre. But some qualifications are in order here. House's TQA model enables us to identify departures between the ST and the TT; but as mentioned earlier these are not necessarily 'errors' in the sense of mistakes in want of rectification. In our example, the omissions are clearly motivated by an intended shift in register and genre, from interpersonal communication to corporate communication. These kinds of shift must be distinguished from genuine errors caused by linguistic incompetence or sheer carelessness on the part of the translator.

Statement of quality

This is critical because it affects the final step in our analysis: producing a 'statement of quality' for the translation. This task can be tricky, for if the so-called errors are not actually mistakes but rather calculated textual moves designed to meet a different purpose (cf. the idea of skopos in Chapter 3), it does not work to simply say unequivocally that a translation is of a good or bad quality. That is the case for our example. The original Chinese report seems to be targeting local, Hong Kong stakeholders and donors, which explains the profusion of gratitude expressions and the higher degree of interpersonal affect: the prospective readers are expected to already be acquainted with the foundation. The Chinese version appeals to this local base and also to the sensibilities of native Chinese users. This goes some way toward explaining why the Chinese text has certain qualities of a speech – it almost sounds like the Chief Campaigner were speaking directly to a local audience, notwithstanding the fact that the text is written in standard Chinese, not in the local dialect.

The English translation, however, possibly targets a foreign and local expatriate readership. These readers are not expected to be familiar with the philanthropic situation in Hong Kong, and the object of the translation would be to acquaint them with the sports charity foundation, hence the corporate flavour in the register of the English version. This could also explain why certain omissions are made, as some segments of the original text may be deemed irrelevant to prospective English readers. In House's terminology, this is called a **covert translation** – a TT that functions like an original text in the TL culture and can be understood within its own terms of reference. This is as opposed to an **overt translation**, a TT that is fixated in the SL culture and cannot be properly understood without reference to the SL context.

A reasonable statement of quality would recognise these differences in target readership and functional purpose between the ST and the

TT and produce a balanced evaluation. In our case, we would say the translation is of a moderately high quality, considering that its clean, undramatic, and direct style would better appeal to the sensibilities of its target readership.

The models presented in this chapter all operate at the level of discourse, hence the discourse paradigm; as far as the study of linguistic structure is concerned, this is the highest rank we can go. In this sense, the discourse paradigm complements the equivalence paradigm, which is primarily concerned with what transpires at the lower ranks of language, such as the word, phrase, or clause. Because the discourse paradigm is theoretically rooted in SFL, it has a strong strain of functionalism in it. It is therefore unsurprising that ideas relating to communicative situations (i.e., the functionalist paradigm) come into play in these theories as well, particularly in Hatim and Mason's register model and House's TQA model. Together these various paradigms constitute an important territory in translation studies that offers prescriptive tools to evaluate translation products, diagnose issues in crosslingual practices, and formulate linguistic solutions to these issues.

Further reading and reflection

1. Read the article 'Shifts of Cohesion and Coherence in Translation' by Shoshana Blum-Kulka (2004). Do you agree with the 'Explicitation Hypothesis', which states that the TT tends to be more cohesive (e.g., by way of installing more linkages between TL clauses), and therefore potentially longer, than the ST? Can you find evidence to the contrary to refute the hypothesis?

2. Read the article '"He 'Catch No Ball' Leh!" Globalization Versus Localization in the Singaporean Translation Market', *Meta* 51(4): 771–786, 2006, by James St. André. The article can be found at: www.erudit.org/en/journals/meta/2006-v51-n4-n4/014341ar/
   a. Within the register model, which element is related to the idea of standard versus nonstandard language?
   b. According to the author, what are the implications of the tension between the local vernacular and standard language for translation practice?
   c. Can you find an example of a similar issue in your culture?

3. So far we have encountered the following conceptual dichotomies:
   a. Formal vs. Dynamic equivalence (Eugene Nida)
   b. Semantic vs. Communicative translation (Peter Newmark)
   c. Documentary vs. Instrumental translation (Christiane Nord)
   d. Domestication vs. Foreignisation (Lawrence Venuti)
   e. Overt vs. Covert translation (Juliane House)
   Look up these terms using the following references: (1) *Dictionary of Translation Studies* (Shuttleworth and Cowie 2014); and (2) *Key Terms in Translation Studies* (Palumbo 2009). Consider the similarities and differences among these concepts in terms of their emphases and implications for translation practice.

5 Beyond the Paradigms

Integrating the paradigms

Now that we have covered the major paradigms and their associated theories in applied translation studies, where do we go from here? One important thing to note is that these paradigms have been treated separately and sequentially to create the sense of a narrative. What we have here is a concise story of how applied translation studies has developed over the past decades, although the theories appear in a chronological order that is not immaculately neat. There is also a spatial logic to this narrative: as we move from the equivalence to the discourse and functionalist paradigms, our unit of analysis expands from the microtextual to the contextual. And context means different things for the discourse and functionalist paradigms: for the former it is principally the co-text, or what is happening beyond the discrete word or expression but within the bounds of the text as an organic whole; the latter on the other hand is interested in the extrinsic setting in which translation is performed and the extraneous factors that impinge on textual operations.

In real-life applications these paradigms operate not in isolation but in tandem. This should already be apparent from the way we have worked through some of our examples. Any act of translating, even in its more extreme manifestation of adaptation, will somehow involve language transfer. So we seldom can escape from the fine-grained treatment of lexis, or the Word – with a capitalised 'w'. This is the province of the equivalence paradigm. But at the same time we almost never work solely with the Word – no sane commissioner would hire someone to translate a singular phrase or sentence, save for advertising slogans or the like. For the most part we deal with a fully fleshed out text, with its array of linguistic means to structure information, connect clauses, register an appropriate tone, and so forth; and with this we enter the realm of the discourse paradigm.

Further: in most cases, an act of translating is motivated and directed *centrifugally*, by which we mean it is undertaken for someone other than the translator, usually to satisfy some external utility. We will recall that a book/movie title or an advertising tagline is not an innocuous, standalone specimen of language; it carries on its shoulders the full burden of a creative idea or marketing campaign. If you are translating a text to fulfil the requirement of your translation course in college, then this translated text is ultimately directed at your professor and for the specific purpose of earning a grade. Even if you are translating a line in your foreign language textbook not for anyone in particular, the act is still considered centrifugal, because here translating serves as a pedagogical means to achieve an end: to master the grammatical structure of a foreign language, and this purpose is extraneous to the act of translating per se.

Of course there are exceptions to this, where one translates merely to derive emotional or somatic satisfaction from the sheer act of translating. Just as one can play a musical piece on an instrument in solitude (not as a practice or rehearsal for some performance), so one can translate for the pleasures of translating, almost in a sadomasochistic sense – this is conceivable especially where literary translation is concerned, where the object of the act is not to hone one's language skills, but to experience the fabric of the ST or the texture of language as such. In these latter cases, translating becomes a *centripetal*, involutionary act: it emanates from and projects itself back unto the translator himself or herself. But we can nonetheless agree that in the majority of cases, translating is an activity driven by some imperative other than self-gratification. This imperative can be political, administrative, economic, social, commercial, and so on. Inasmuch as some such external imperative is in place, translation becomes a purposive and goal-driven activity, and the functionalist paradigm is set in motion.

All three paradigms can therefore converge on a single translating event. We have seen quite a few examples of this, particularly in Chapters 3 and 4, but let us just cite one final case here: court interpreting. We have not been mentioning interpreting (oral translating) very much because it is usually seen as another subfield of its own. But within the broad rubric of applied studies, interpreting shares common features with other modes of translation. Needless to say, interpreting for the law requires a high measure of equivalence – and usually of the literal rather than dynamic or communicative variety. The interpreter's focused attention on the semantics and nuance of the exact words used as well as the delivery of those words is crucial; a material deviation from the original utterance in both content and manner (i.e., what a party to litigation says and also how it is said) can have immense implications for the legal proceedings in a bilingual or multilingual jurisdiction.

But things are much more complicated than that. Interpreters work with their clients and with the court system, which means they are executing a translatorial act within a wider discursive event. The UK-based professional interpreter Sue Leschen relates her experience of translating for a court in Northern Ireland, where some laws and regulations differ from England. As part of her preparation work in one assignment, she

> requested advance disclosure of the pleadings in the case (statements and other documents filed by the parties with the court) but to no avail due to 'confidentiality' ... All that the agency [who hired the interpreter's service] was able to obtain from the Northern Ireland court service was the wording of the charge under the relevant NI [Northern Ireland] Order. (Leschen 2016b: 20)

This suggests that an interpreter has to deal with not just texts, but also various parties and institutions. At one point, Leschen (2016b: 21) had to notify the judge that she could not hear the counsel and jury properly because of where she was seated, thereafter microphones and headphones were installed. Based on Leschen's (2016a) anecdotal accounts, we can glean some functionalist aspects of her work. She may be obliged to participate in the client's strategy meetings with witnesses. Overnight reading 'is always necessary in long-running court cases'; this is especially so when dealing with areas of law with which she is unfamiliar, which meant 'working extremely hard each night to check [her] understanding of the legal issues and terminology involved'. She often has to 'read reams of statements and reports in readiness for the next day's hearing'. In one assignment, because her request for prior disclosure of pleadings had been rejected, she 'had to digest all the French and English pleadings ... on arrival in the court' (21). This confirms what we have learnt about the interactive aspect of translatorial action and also the role of research in professional translating.

On one assignment in Guernsey, a British Crown Dependency that is not part of the UK, Leschen had to familiarise herself

> with a certain amount of specialist terminology, such as 'Bailiwicks (jurisdictions) of Jersey and Guernsey' ... This was in addition to my usual preparation of the particular legal terminology involved in each case, based on the (limited) advanced information provided by the courts. Fortunately, after 16 years' experience of interpreting in the courts, I have legal terminology banks at my finger tips, and being a qualified lawyer gives me a head start every time. (Leschen 2016a: 20)

Legal terminology falls under the Field domain in our register model. On her assignment in Northern Ireland, Leschen (2016b: 21) notes that the barristers 'spoke at a manageable speed, with one notable exception, who delivered huge chunks of information without seeming to pause for breath'. Further,

> the defendant's French was heavily accented, as it was her second language and she had apparently never lived in France ...
> All of the legal personnel spoke English with strong Northern Ireland accents, peppered with such gems as 'wee girl' and exclamations like 'ock!'. Their political stance was revealed by clues such as their use of 'Londonderry' (used by unionists) versus 'Derry' (generally favoured by Irish nationalists). (Leschen 2016b: 21)

In the parlance of the register model, speed and accent are particular to speech and therefore comes under Mode; the use of sociolects to express political stance, on the other hand, is an instantiation of Tenor.

Beyond the word

The equivalence, functionalist, and discourse paradigms deal primarily with textual data. We have also on occasion taken into account nonverbal elements as well as how these elements interact with language proper to produce signification in a holistic communicative event. Nonverbal elements feature particularly strongly in advertising translation, audiovisual translation, and website localisation, where meaning is communicated by way of multiple modes and media. In general terms, mode relates to our sense faculties, that is to say, whether a piece of communication is primarily verbal, visual, aural, kinetic, or synaesthetic; medium, on the other hand, pertains to the material-technological platform that embodies a piece of communication, as, for example, the difference between a website, a printed book, and a work of architecture. The distinction between the two notions, however, may be blurred at times, and a change in media almost always entails a change in mode.

Where acts of communication traverse boundaries, be they modal, medial, or cultural-linguistic, can we reimagine these acts as translational? This may be a conceptual question, but to the degree that it affects the way we think and speak about our daily communications (which often cross boundaries), it is also a question with practical implications. The theme of crossing different types of boundary is immanent in Roman Jakobson's tripartite typology of interlingual, intralingual, and intersemiotic translation (see p.72), and at various points in our preceding discussion we have come across these various formations of translation. To recapitulate: while the idea of intersemioticity implies the crossing over from one mode and/or medium into another, that of intralinguality reminds us that a language or culture is seldom a monolithic slab, and may involve crossings within itself. These ideas enrich the fabric of what we ordinarily call translation (i.e., in the interlingual sense) and affords us a metaphorical rubric with which we can rehash the nature of our communications.

In summary, not only can a text traverse the space *between* languages and cultures, it can move *within* them; the same pattern works for mode and medium: there can be an *inter-* and an *intra-* dimension. What happens when we let these vectors interact with and intersect one another? We get a translational matrix, such as the one shown in Table 5.1.

The model presented in Table 5.1 is an inclusive one, and illustrates the potential of translation to metamorphose itself within the interplay – and also *intraplay*, if we could coin a new term – of mode/medium and language/culture. Translation can therefore be more than what the lay person thinks it is. Our translational imaginary should stretch beyond the movement of texts across languages, even beyond text and language as such, to take into its view other kinds of transaction that characterise our communications. This does not mean discarding conventional notions of translating and extending translation infinitely and irrevocably toward abstraction. The attitude we advocate for applied translation

Table 5.1 A translational matrix

Type	Intracultural	Transcultural
Intramodal	Translating within a culture in the same mode, e.g., translating a German play into Viennese	Translating across cultures in the same mode, e.g., translating Disney comics into Japanese *manga*
Intermodal	Translating within a culture from one mode to a different mode, e.g., translating a picture manual into a text manual	Translating across cultures from one mode to a different mode, e.g., translating a Bible text into a comic in a different language
Intramedial	Translating within a culture in the same medium, e.g., adapting American music videos for a Spanish-speaking audience in the USA	Translating across cultures in the same medium, e.g., translating a French *opéra comique* into a German Romantic opera
Intermedial	Translating within a culture from one medium to a different medium, e.g., adapting a novel into a film in the same language	Translating across cultures from one medium to a different medium, e.g., transformation of a play into a musical in a different language

Source: Kaindl (2013: 261–262); the table format is mine.

studies is to acknowledge the continuing value of the equivalence, functionalist, and discourse paradigms, while keeping an open mind to **the translational**; in other words: textual and non-textual practices that can count as embodying the concept of translation, and which may or may not involve translating in the everyday sense of the word.

The translational: From translation to translanguaging

We have established that any interlingual or crosscultural event can integrate the different paradigms of applied translation studies, and also that the translational constitutes a matrix of complex intersections between mode/medium and language/culture. We now proceed to inter-rogate the idea of translational applications beyond the paradigms; in other words, is there an applied dimension to translation studies beyond praxis, beyond the technicalities of translating? In respect of photography, the author John Berger remarks:

> There is a widespread assumption that if one is interested in the visual, one's interest must be limited to a technique of somehow *treating* the visual. Thus the visual is divided into categories of special interest: painting, photography, real appearances, dreams and so on. And what is forgotten – like all essential questions in a positivist culture – is the meaning and enigma of visibility itself. (Berger 2013: 43)

In an analogical way, is our interest in translation, to appropriate Berger's terms, limited to techniques of treating the textual? The analogy with the visual seems plausible, considering translation theory too is rather obsessed with 'categories of special interest': we have been looking at manifestations of the textual in various genres and text types, and how they should be differentially *treated* in translation. But have we, as Berger says of the visual, forgotten the essence of textuality or the translational itself?

A systematic study of translation involves more than checking all the theoretical boxes and slotting textual phenomena into those boxes. In fact, we do not have all the boxes here: the survey undertaken in this book does not purport to be comprehensive and exhaustive, though we have covered sufficient grounds to appreciate and reason through pertinent issues. But ultimately what we are doing here is not all about theories; it is also about attuning ourselves into a *translational sensibility*, into our **languaged** world, as well as cultivating a heightened sensitivity and nuanced response to it. In other words, applied translation studies is not just about applying established theories of translation; it is just as much about recognising, appreciating, and thinking translation in all its creative and critical potentialities in our everyday lives. Let us look at three brief examples in this connection.

My first example draws upon David Crystal's understanding of the phenomenon called **textese**. Often associated with the advent of mobile technology (although its concept can be traced back at least to the nineteenth century), this is a register of writing that inflects our normal written language through phonetic reduction of orthodox spelling and substitution of numbers for letters, as for example, *C u l8r* ('see you later'). Textese can be used to translate book or film titles, as in *ChRIE &*

t chocl8 factorE, from 'Charlie and the Chocolate Factory' and *Alice in 1derl&*, from 'Alice in Wonderland' (Crystal 2010: 193). Such linguistic experimentation is not limited to English, of course. In French, *merci* ('thank you', pronounced *mare-see*) is spelled by texters (people sending text messages) as *mr6* because the French word for 'six' sounds like 'see'; in German, *achtung* ('attention') is spelled as *8ung*, where the number 8 substitutes *acht*, which means 'eight' in German; in Spanish, *saludos* means 'greetings', and this is often abbreviated into *salu2*, where the *dos* (meaning 'two' in Spanish) gets kicked out by the numeral; and in Welsh, *nawr*, which means 'now', is *9r*, and of course this is because 'nine' is *naw* in Welsh (194).

With these examples, Crystal drives home the point that the advent of texting, with all the truncations and deformations that it brings to modern English, would not result in a deterioration in users' proficiency, as many language practitioners might worry. The basic argument is that you need to know how to spell a word properly in the first place before you can insert a numeral or symbol in the appropriate place; hence: 'the best texters are also the best spellers' (Crystal 2010: 192). The less conservative view on textese is that its use triggers innovation and evolution in the English language. For our purposes, these samples of textese serve to exemplify intersemioticity, where language users creatively appropriate the *slippage* between alphabets and numerals or symbols as well as between their orthography (visual) and phonetics (aural) to produce novel and imaginative formations of language.

Textese is highly performative, used not merely for speed and convenience, but also for shaping a discursive identity in the world of virtual communications; and as we have seen, textese can also turn into a quasi-code, a linguistic game of sorts, to translate otherwise ordinary pieces of language. This is not translation in the conventional sense, we concede, but it is nonetheless *translational* in that it embodies transfer and transformation between different modalities of communication. On this account, textese is an excellent illustration of what is called **translanguaging** (García & Li 2014), a concept that encapsulates various kinds of transaction operating *between and beyond* languages and emanating a sense of creativity and/or criticality.

My second example comes from an artefact. Figure 5.1 shows a 'red packet' that the Chinese people use during the Lunar New Year, where, as a ritualised custom, people put a nominal amount of money into

Figure 5.1 A Lunar New Year red packet. Author's photograph

the envelope and give it to their relatives and friends (normally from seniors to juniors) to convey their good wishes. The one in Figure 5.1 is designed in Hong Kong. In the first instance, the words on the red packet are extremely jarring: *Wish you FAT LIKE A PIG HEAD.* This certainly does not sound like a very nice blessing; if anything it sounds like an ironic insult. A foreigner (including a non-local Chinese person) in Hong Kong would rightly feel offended upon receiving a red packet like this – unless of course the monetary content in it is attractive enough to compensate for the apparent insolence of the words!

We could call the image in Figure 5.1 a **translational text**, that is, a text that is not prima facie a piece of translation but which nonetheless incorporates elements of translation into its constitution. In this example, 'fat like a pig head' is a partial transliteration and a partial calque – two translation techniques we have come across. 'Fat' is a transliteration of the Cantonese *faat*, which means to gain wealth, and therefore an auspicious word. 'Like a pig head' is a morpheme-for-morpheme translation of a colloquial Cantonese expression that means exactly the same thing on the face of the English words, but with very a positive connotation in the local dialect – 'pig head' here is a metaphor for fullness or wholesomeness; this is rooted in the traditional folk imagination that wealthy people are typically plump because they can afford to eat very well. The expression on the whole basically means to be wealthy and prosperous.

It so happens that the transliterated Cantonese word 'fat' can both orthographically and phonetically conflate with the English word 'fat' (in an approximate way), generating a rich, layered sign. It is a palimpsest that points the bilingual reader in two different directions, hence producing a very localised form of humour. Note that not all Chinese readers would be able to get the word play: a Chinese person not acquainted with the vernacular in Hong Kong would be as clueless as an English speaker as to what this expression is about.

In this short piece of discourse, we see a creative interplay of language that embeds within it a clandestine translational operation. The whole text can be read in English throughout, possibly heading toward a repugnant interpretation. But beneath this surface form there is a translingual expression leading from the English 'Wish you' to a calqued Cantonese phrase, mediated through the anomalous, double-tiered English–Cantonese sign 'Fat'. This is translanguaging at work, where ingredients from two languages are used in a resourceful and creative manner to convey meaning – in this case a New Year blessing.

Our third example is a commercial product in the form of a brand of craft beer known as *gweilo*, manufactured and trademarked in Hong Kong. The locale is relevant here, for the term *gweilo* speaks directly to the history of Hong Kong, a British colony for about 150 years. The term, a transliteration from Cantonese, literally means 'ghost man' and is a derogatory reference to foreigners (Westerners specifically) used by the ethnic Chinese in Hong Kong, though in the local vernacular today, it has lost much of its pejorative tone. It may be of interest that *gweilo*, having entered the *Oxford English Dictionary*, is now part of the modern English repertoire via borrowing.

Figure 5.2 shows the company's signature label, which appears on all their beer bottles. It has the semblance of a dictionary entry but subverts it. As we move down the definitions, we are taken through linguistics and history to commerce: the last definition about the brand and the beer, of course, embodies the real message. What is interesting about this label is that, against the visuality of a pseudo-dictionary – the Chinese characters, the phonetic transcription, the abbreviated grammatical descriptions, and the numerical sequence of the definitions (starting from the literal to the abstract) – it tells us not to treat it with absolute seriousness. It is tongue-in-cheek, insinuating an element of mischief into the aura of a dictionary form, and that is why it works so well as a piece of marketing communication.

Is there applied translation in here? Yes, there is. In the first place the choice of *gweilo* as a brand name is strategic in Hong Kong's sociohistorical context, as the transliterated term sits at the interface of East–West culture, at the edge of translatability. It is therefore a site of **cultural translation**, defined here as all the exchanges and interactions, including acts of translating, that occur when one culture encounters another. The image of the dictionary entry is therefore pertinent, for it brings forth the *concept of translation* (incorporating some actual translation in the text itself), appropriated and transformed into a clever tactic that relates the product to the intercultural dynamic of its target market.

The preceding examples demonstrate how one might look at applied translation studies from a different angle. Translation can be *applied* in the sense of *doing* the act of translating – this is a trite definition by now; or it can be applied in the sense of being insinuated into our lives at various levels and on a daily basis, such as in text messaging practices, creative marketing communications, and in many other arenas. This is where translation blends into translanguaging, and vice versa, in *mundane* textual practices. I emphasise 'mundane' because part of what we

Figure 5.2 A beer bottle label. Reproduced with permission from Gweilo Beer (Hong Kong) Limited.

Source: http://gweilobeer.com

mean by applied translation studies lies in teasing out the translational from commonplace discursive-semiotic events, particularly in superdiverse, multilingual cities. This dimension of applied translation complements skill-based translating, based on the three paradigms discussed in this book, thereby placing translating alongside other affiliated language practices that provide creative and critical resources for communication.

Moving on from the applied: Conceptual articulations

Within the larger picture of translation studies as an academic inquiry, the various paradigms in applied translation studies represent early attempts at making the field systematic and scientific. This by no means suggests that applied translation studies is now out of fashion. But as a matter of historical fact, it is important to know that some of the assumptions underlying the prescriptive paradigms we have been looking at were strongly criticised in the 1980s when academics started to investigate translational phenomena from a non-prescriptive point of view. The year 1985 saw the publication of a seminal work that heralded conceptual translation studies. Entitled *The Manipulation of Literature*, this is a collection of essays (republished in 2014) by an international cluster of scholars active since the mid-1970s, including Theo Hermans, Susan Bassnett, André Lefevere, Gideon Toury, José Lambert, and Maria Tymoczko, among others – collectively known as the **Manipulation School**. Its name derived from the book's title, the 'School' is in fact bound only in terms of a generalised research spirit. The above scholars were dissatisfied with the state of the discipline at the time, dominated as it was by largely prescriptive theories, and set themselves the task of reforming its fundamental goals and methodologies. They reconsidered the efficacy of traditional conceptions of (mainly literary) translation, and critiqued them for installing an original text as an 'exalted, untouchable, inimitable, hallowed' entity, and condemning translation 'as a foolhardy and barely permissible undertaking, doomed from the start and to be judged, at best, in terms of relative fidelity, and at worst as outright sacrilege' (Hermans 2014: 7–8). In response to this, the Manipulation School espoused instead

a view of literature as a complex and dynamic *system*; a conviction that there should be a continual *interplay* between theoretical models and practical case studies; an approach to literary translation which is *descriptive, target-oriented, functional and systemic*; and an interest in the *norms and constraints* that govern the production and reception of translations, in the *relation* between translation and other types of text processing, and in the *place and role* of translations both within a given literature and in the *interaction* between literatures. (Hermans 2014: 10–11; emphasis added)

These are the foundational concepts of a new tradition that would alter the course of contemporary translation studies. In contradistinction to earlier approaches, this tradition is marked by its *conceptual-descriptive* rather than *applied-prescriptive* stance. This book has covered linguistics-oriented paradigms in translation, based on transformational-generative linguistics (the equivalence paradigm), communication theories (the functionalist paradigm), and Hallidayan linguistics (the discourse paradigm). These approaches are largely normative in that their principal objective is to provide guiding principles and assessment criteria in respect of translating; they are applied in nature insofar as their theoretical apparatuses are aimed at producing the optimum end-product. Although the specifics of each theory may differ, they are all in a way future-oriented, for they are interested in diagnosis and prescription, that is, *how it should be done*, rather than, say, *why it is done the way it was done*. The latter question, which involves description and explanation, as opposed to assessment and evaluation, is taken up by what can be called the **systems paradigm**.

The systems paradigm, pioneered by Itamar Even-Zohar and Gideon Toury, is expressly not interested in prescription: it does not tell us how to translate, why an utterance should not be translated in this or that way, or why a certain ST should be deemed untranslatable. Under the systems paradigm, the end-product of translation, and hence its translatability, is already a given to start with. The task of the systems theorist is not to judge the quality of the translation output, but to investigate into the circumstances of its production, circulation, and reception, with an interest in such themes as systems, relations, norms, constraints, roles, and interactions (see Herman's quote above). These correlated themes amassed into Even-Zohar's theoretical framework, **polysystem theory**, a theory which views literary translation as a tiered system operating under a set of norms, interacting with other tiered systems, such as politics and economics, within a culture. They were further made operational by a methodology by Gideon Toury, which constituted (and still does) something of a subfield, known as **descriptive translation studies** (DTS).

Based on empirical and/or historical data and a relatively scientific methodology, this paradigm has become the dominant model since the mid-1980s whose influence can still be felt today. It is the theoretical engine behind the cultural 'turn' in the field, briefly mentioned in Chapter 1, spurring the emergence of the **cultural-ideological paradigm**. This paradigm draws upon the resources and counter-hegemonic orientation of the cultural studies field. Susan Bassnett and André Lefevere were the pioneering scholars who advocated the reconceptualisation of translation as an ideological act, laden with values of all kinds, infested with manipulations both within the translated text and without, such that all translations are essentially a form of **rewriting**. The task of the translation scholar, according to this view, is to elucidate the ideological underpinnings of the translation product and expose the unequal power relations simmering beneath the surface of an apparently innocuous act of translation.

There are many strands within the cultural 'turn', the most prominent of which include **postcolonial translation studies** (PTS) and **feminist translation studies** (FTS). Even though these lines of inquiry derive their theoretical bases from the descriptive tradition, they also depart from that tradition in their espousal of strong political agendas, with the first challenging Anglo-American cultural hegemony and the second challenging patriarchal hegemony. The more pertinent point for us is that both of these conceptual theories are at the same time manifestly applied, in the sense that their political agendas are realised not through pure argumentation but through specific forms of praxis.

Feminist translation scholars, for example, do not just talk about their resistance toward male-centred discourses; they also *perform* their ideas through **agentive translations**, that is, translations that manipulate orthographic details of language to flaunt a feminist positionality: a simple example in English would be to deliberately reconstrue *his*tory as *her*story, or to coin a neologism such as *womankind* to take a dig at the word '*man*kind' – although the same would probably not be done for the words '*man*hunt' and '*man*slaughter'. The applied dimension of FTS comes into high relief through their advocacy of interventionist procedures, culminating in what is called the **feminist translation project**. These projects are activist in nature, ranging from translating (and subverting perceived masculinist manifestations in) literary texts, localising web content with a feminist twist, disseminating feminist writings across languages, to effecting socially embedded transnational movements (see Castro & Ergun 2017: section III 'Feminist Translation in Action'). The importance of translating as praxis in the context of feminism is epitomised in the following comments by Judith Butler:

I think there can be no solidarity without translation, and certainly no global solidarity ... It matters that we start with linguistic translation, since dominant terms such as 'gender' and even 'difference' itself do not necessarily translate. Or when they do translate, they become new words, entering into a different set of linguistic histories and associations ... The more important task is to let the dominant language be disrupted by those languages generally regarded as marginal, or not regarded at all. More important

164 : APPLIED TRANSLATION STUDIES

than agreeing on a single language for feminism is the *development of a set of translation practices that do not simply reproduce colonial or imperial logics.* (Cited in Nagar et al. 2017: 113; emphasis added)

Butler's call for FTS to devise 'a set of translation practices that do not simply reproduce colonial or imperial logics' finds a neat echo in PTS, whose fiercest exponent is Lawrence Venuti. We have already come across Venuti's signature notion of domestication versus foreignisation (see p.68), which, notwithstanding their conceptual-ideological thrust, are fundamentally practical approaches to translating. Like FTS, Venuti's theory seeks to *change the world,* or at least some aspect of it (especially pertinent here is the title of his 2012 work: *Translation Changes Everything*), by advancing, as well as practising, radical methods of translating. In the case of Venuti, foreignisation leads to stilted, SL-flavoured translations designed to pull the TT reader inexorably back to the linguistic and cultural Other, and hence is at least as much applied as it is conceptual.

An extended example of how Venuti's theory is instantiated in practice, in this case the theatre, is found in the AHRC Leadership Fellowship Project, 'Translating Theatre: "Foreignisation" on Stage' (2016–2018). The project begins with Venuti's premise and experiments with his theory through embodied practice – as opposed to, for instance, purely intellectual contemplation:

Translation scholar Lawrence Venuti argues that translation is always already an act of domestication, but champions 'foreignisation', an ethical effect on target readers that translators can seek to generate in order to limit the degree to which the unfamiliar is forcibly turned into the familiar, silencing cultural difference. How 'foreignisation' is achieved depends on the context in which the translation will be received. A set of discursive and non-discursive strategies – such as the choice of source texts that do not conform to dominant taste and expectations in the target context – need to be considered alongside performance elements such as casting, acting, mise en scène, performance style, design, music/sound, costumes, and so on. Despite the recent academic interest in 'foreignisation', theatre studies still lack a debate on what seeking a 'foreignising' effect would mean for text and performance, and whether theatre – as opposed to literature – requires a distinctive approach. (www.translatingtheatre.com/the-project/)

The project thus sets itself the task of investigating what a foreignising approach to theatre translation or adaptation might look like; whether foreignisation works well for different kinds of textual sources; the effects of 'foreignisation' on performance and mise en scène; how a foreignising translation is negotiated by theatre practitioners; and how audiences respond to this kind of translation. The project team, led by Margherita Laera, translated three plays into English: *Black Tenderness*, written in Spanish by Denise Despeyroux and translated by Simon Breden; *The Snakes*, written in French by Marie Ndiaye and translated by Kélina Gotman; and *Gliwice Hamlet*, written in Polish by Piotr Lachmann and translated by Aneta Mancewicz and Bryce Lease. The translations, however, were not executed in conventional (read: domesticated) style. In alignment with Venuti's theoretical position, the translators' discursive strategies converged on the following (see www.translating theatre.com/video-archive/):

1. Tracing the syntactical structure of the SL to retain the way thoughts are being structured in the original language of composition. For example, Simon Breden deliberately retains long run-on sentences in the Spanish play *Black Tenderness*, with its preponderance of subclauses and prepositional phrases, as well as Latin structures where verbs are often pushed back. All of this creates a defamiliarising effect in English.
2. Retaining colloquial and idiomatic turns of phrases. For example, the Polish idiom *idę po trupach*, literally 'I walk over corpses', was rendered as such into English despite – or rather precisely because of – its awkwardness, rather than translated sense-for-sense as 'to do something at any cost'; for the Spanish expression *voy volando*, which can be rendered more idiomatically as 'I'm on my way' or 'I'll be there in a flash', Breden chooses to retain in his translation the kinetic image of flying (*volando*) in the Spanish, hence: 'I'll fly to you.'
3. Linking the choice of apparently ordinary words to the tone of the play. Thus, for Kélina Gotman, the French *on* (equivalent to the pronoun 'one' in English, though it can also mean 'we'), as in *on va faire ceci ou cela* ('one is going to do this or that'), does not translate well as 'you', despite this being a most convenient solution, as she deems the English 'you' too personal to render the impersonality of *on* and also the cold, detached ambience of the play *The Snakes*.

4. Sensitising oneself to the phonetics of the SL. For example, in *Gliwice Hamlet*, there is the Polish expression *sierpień-cierpień* ('August-suffering'), which describes the kind of suffering one experiences during August due to the summer heat. Directly translating this as 'August suffering' would lose the acoustic quality of the ST. Aneta Mancewicz and Bryce Lease opt instead for the phrase 'summer suffering' to inject a sibilance while still keeping the semantics of heat and misery.

What is significant about this experimental project is the conscious application of a translation theory on theatrical translation, the practical manifestations of which can be seen in the above examples. The entire project team, including the researchers, producers, actors/ actresses, and translators, have all read Venuti's work before embarking on their work, such that the notion of foreignisation is adopted as a systematic approach to produce estrangement in translated theatre. This bearing of translation theory on translating is best encapsulated in Kélina Gotman's remarks in her interview, where she says theory has given her the 'licence' to take bolder decisions, particularly to maintain the alterity of the SL, and to not 'censor' herself in allowing the structure of the French 'to carry' the English language.

Foreignisation has also become the umbrella concept of the entire project – that of 'staging otherness', in other words, 'to minimise the translated text's integration within the target language's standard dialect, and instead to communicate its linguistic and cultural difference' (Pitrolo 2017: 7). Beyond language, foreignisation also figures in other aspects of dramatic art, such as the mise en scène and casting, aligning with Bertolt Brecht's famous notion of *Verfremdungseffekt* (alienation effect). It is here that we can see the potential for practice to refine theory (Venuti's own illustrations are mainly from literature), thereby producing synergy between the applied and the conceptual.

At an even higher level, the Translating Theatre project was conceived with the referendum on Brexit in mind. Through a foreignised approach to theatrical translation, it seeks to 'contribute to the debate on how UK theatre culture deals with the presence of the "foreign" in its representational economy' (Pitrolo 2017: 9). At this sensitive point in time 'when immigration is at the centre of the political agenda and nationalist, anti-European sentiments are on the rise', foreignisation in theatre translation, with its implications for how we know/represent the cultural Other and its dialectic with the now commonplace notion of cultural translation, can indeed 'offer a public arena for intercultural dialogue' (www.translatingtheatre.com/the-project/). This suggests to us that the significance of the research project extends beyond theatre translation; its material outcomes (the translated plays) have the potential to be extrapolated to a critical understanding of contemporary society and politics, possibly with a view to effecting changes.

This last point about effecting changes is crucial. We can see Venuti's theory, indeed FTS as well, as being applied in the sense that they deal head-on with events happening 'on the ground', and not just contemplatively but in activist fashion. Unlike polysystem theory, which purports to predict translation behaviour, Venuti lashes out directly at what he perceives to be unjust in the world of translation and actively proposes to make things right (and also demonstrates how to do that through his own translations).

For example, one of his criticisms is against the stark asymmetry between Anglophone and non-Anglophone markets in the volume of published translations, including literary ones. Venuti (2008) reports that among the large volume of new books brought out annually by US and UK publishers, translated books take up only between 2 and 4 per cent. Contrast this to the publication figures in other Western European countries, where the proportion of translations within the total book output is significantly higher: between 20 and 26 per cent in Italy, between 8 and 12 per cent in France, and between 7 and 14 per cent in Germany (11). In the specific domain of poetry, the figures are comparable: 5–8 per cent in the USA versus more than 13 per cent in Italy (Venuti 2012: 173). To Venuti (2012), Anglophone practices of marginalising translation 'are questionable not merely because they have admitted relatively few foreign texts from a narrow range of foreign cultures, but also because they have formed aggressively monolingual readerships in the United Kingdom and the United States, generally uninterested in translations' (158–159).

Strictly speaking there is nothing too conceptual about this observation; if anything it is political, fully grounded in reality based on statistics from the publishing industry, and constitutes the basis for shifting such reality toward a more balanced state of affairs. While polysystem theory is a classic conceptual theory in that it is driven by empirical data to generate explanatory findings, Venuti *drives new empirical data* by producing translations of his own while simultaneously lobbying for the increased visibility of translators and of the translation profession more generally. His theory can be considered 'applied' by virtue of directly engaging with and also potentially feeding back into our empirical realities.

In Chapter 1 it was mentioned that the applied and the conceptual represent two quite different but equally meaningful facets in the field of translation studies. Postcolonial and feminist articulations of translation exemplify this fluidity of the applied-conceptual divide, suggesting perhaps that we can nuance the distinction between the two. Some conceptual theories are indeed in the ivory tower (and there is nothing wrong with that); apart from polysystem theory, there is the **sociological paradigm**, which examines translators' orientations against the background of all the relevant indicia in their personal and professional trajectory, in particular the values they have inculcated in the course of their education and socialisation. These theories are valuable as academic, intellectual resources. Others, like FTS and (Venuti's strand of) PTS, are more 'hands-on': they do not just describe and analyse, they translate and critique translations in a way that raises controversy and hence converge attention on the problem at hand, with a view to filling gaps and reversing imbalances.

The rest, as they always say, is history. Despite how far the field has moved on, we hold dear to our three paradigms that are the foundation of applied translation studies. Though historical in terms of chronological time, they are still contemporary by way of their deep involvement in the daily business of our multilingual lives. It is for this reason that applied translation studies will continue to thrive alongside more recent and also future theoretical developments in the field.

Bibliography

Alfer, Alexa (2015) 'Transcending Boundaries', *The Linguist* 54(5): 26–27.

Baker, Mona (2011) *In Other Words: A Coursebook on Translation* (Second Edition), Abingdon: Routledge.

Baker, Mona and Gabriela Saldanha (eds) (2009) *Routledge Encyclopedia of Translation Studies* (Second Edition), Abingdon: Routledge.

Bennett, Karen (2007) 'Epistemicide! The Tale of a Predatory Discourse', *The Translator* 13(2): 151–169.

Bennett, Karen (2013) 'English as a Lingua Franca in Academia', *The Interpreter and Translator Trainer* 7(2): 169–193.

Berger, John (2013) *Understanding a Photograph*, London: Penguin.

Berman, Antoine (2012 [1985]) 'Translation and the Trials of the Foreign', trans. Lawrence Venuti, in Lawrence Venuti (ed.) *The Translation Studies Reader* (Third Edition), Abingdon: Routledge, 240–253.

Blum-Kulka, Shoshana (2004) 'Shifts of Cohesion and Coherence in Translation', in Lawrence Venuti (ed.) *The Translation Studies Reader* (Second Edition), Abingdon: Routledge, 290–305.

Brown, Allison (2015) 'Re-writing History', *The Linguist* 54(5): 13–15.

Castro, Olga and Emek Ergun (eds) (2017) *Feminist Translation Studies: Local and Transnational Perspectives*, Abingdon: Routledge.

Catford, J. C. (1965) *A Linguistic Theory of Translation: An Essay in Applied Linguistics*, London: Oxford University Press.

Chartered Institute of Linguists (2016) 'A Glass Half Full', *The Linguist* 55(5): 22–23.

Chesterman, Andrew and Emma Wagner (2014) *Can Theory Help Translators? A Dialogue Between the Ivory Tower and the Wordface*, Abingdon: Routledge.

Cheung, Martha P. Y. (2014) 'Translation as Intercultural Communication: Views from the Chinese Discourse on Translation', in Sandra Bermann and Catherine Porter (eds), *A Companion to Translation Studies*, Chichester: Wiley Blackwell.

Clayton, Gwen (2015) 'The Law of Japan', *The Linguist* 54(2): 16–17.

Cole, Brendan (2016) 'The Bard in Chinese', *The Linguist* 55(1): 18–19.

Crystal, David (2010) *A Little Book of Language*, New Haven, CT: Yale University Press.

Deeter, Michelle (2015) 'A Patent Challenge', *The Linguist* 54(1): 14–15.

Duff, Alan (1981) *The Third Language: Recurrent Problems of Translation into English*, Oxford: Pergamon Press.

Freiburg, Ilse (2015) 'Posing the Right Questions', *The Linguist* 54(2): 11–13.

Gambier, Yves and Luc van Doorslaer (2010) *Handbook of Translation Studies*, Vol. 1, Amsterdam: John Benjamins.

García, Ofelia and Li Wei (2014) *Translanguaging: Language, Bilingualism and Education*, Basingstoke: Palgrave.

Gentzler, Edwin (2001) *Contemporary Translation Studies* (Second Edition), Clevedon: Multilingual Matters.

Halliday, Michael A. K. and Ruqaiya Hasan (1976) *Cohesion in English*, London: Longman.

Hatim, Basil and Ian Mason (1990) *Discourse and the Translator*, London: Routledge.

Hatim, Basil and Ian Mason (1997) *The Translator as Communicator*, London: Routledge.

Hermans, Theo (2014) *The Manipulation of Literature: Studies in Literary Translation,* Abingdon: Routledge.

Ho, George (2004) 'Translating Advertisements across Heterogeneous Cultures', *The Translator* 10(2): 221–243.

House, Juliane (2015) *Translation Quality Assessment: Past and Present*, Abingdon: Routledge.

InspiringHK Sports Foundation (2016) *2015–2016 Impact Report*, Hong Kong: InspiringHK Sports Foundation.

Jakobson, Roman (2012 [1959]) 'On Linguistic Aspects of Translation', in Lawrence Venuti (ed.) *The Translation Studies Reader* (Third Edition), Abingdon: Routledge, 126–131.

Kaindl, Klaus (2013) 'Multimodality and Translation', in Carmen Millán and Francesca Bartrina (eds) *The Routledge Handbook of Translation Studies*, Abingdon: Routledge, 257–269.

Klaudy, Kinga (2001) 'The Asymmetry Hypothesis. Testing the Asymmetric Relationship between Explicitations and Implicitations', Paper presented to the Third International Congress of EST 'Claims, Changes and Challenges in Translation Studies', Copenhagen, 30 August–1 September 2001.

Leschen, Sue (2016a) 'Channel Vision', *The Linguist* 55(4): 20–21.

Leschen, Sue (2016b) 'Northern Ireland: Day in Court', *The Linguist* 55(6): 20–21.

Macdonald, James (2015) *Why Globalization Fails: The Rise and Fall of Pax Americana*, New York: Farrar, Straus and Giroux.

Munday, Jeremy (2009) *The Routledge Companion to Translation Studies* (Revised Edition), Abingdon: Routledge.

Myers-Scotton, Carol (2006) *Multiple Voices: An Introduction to Bilingualism*, Malden, MA: Blackwell.

Nagar, Richa, Kathy Davis, Judith Butler, Analouise Keating, Claudia de Lima Costa, Sonia E. Alvarez, and Ayşe Gül Altinay (2017) 'A Cross-Disciplinary Roundtable on the Feminist Politics of Translation', in Olga Castro and Emek Ergun (eds) *Feminist Translation Studies: Local and Transnational Perspectives*, Abingdon: Routledge, 111–135.

Nida, Eugene A. (1964) *Toward a Science of Translating: With Special Reference to Principles and Procedures Involved in Bible Translating*, Leiden: E.J. Brill.

Nida, Eugene A. (2003) *Fascinated By Languages*, Amsterdam: John Benjamins.

Nida, Eugene A. and Charles R. Taber (1969) *The Theory and Practice of Translation*, Leiden: Brill.

Newmark, Peter (1988) *A Textbook of Translation*, Hertfordshire: Prentice Hall.

Nord, Christiane (2014) *Translating as a Purposeful Activity: Functionalist Approaches Explained*, Abingdon: Routledge.

Olohan, Maeve (2016) *Scientific and Technical Translation*, Abingdon: Routledge.

Palumbo, Giuseppe (2009) *Key Terms in Translation Studies*, London: Continuum.

Pennycook, Alastair and Emi Otsuji (2015) *Metrolingualism: Language in the City*, Abingdon: Routledge.

Perales-Escudero, Moisés and John M. Swales (2011) 'Tracing Convergence and Divergence in Pairs of Spanish and English Research Article Abstracts: The Case of *Ibérica*', *Ibérica* 21: 49–70.

Pitrolo, Flora (2017) 'Staging Otherness', *The Linguist* 56(3): 7–9.

Pym, Anthony (2004) *The Moving Text: Localization, Translation, and Distribution*, Amsterdam: John Benjamins.

Pym, Anthony (2011) 'Website Localization', in Kirsten Malmkjær and Kevin Windle (eds) *The Oxford Handbook of Translation Studies*, Oxford: Oxford University Press, 410–424.

Pym, Anthony (2014) *Exploring Translation Theories* (Second Edition), Abingdon: Routledge.

Reiss, Katharina (1989 [1977]) 'Text-types, Translation Types and Translation Assessment', translated by Andrew Chesterman, in Andrew Chesterman (ed.) *Readings in Translation Theory*, Helsinki: Finn Lectura, 105–115.

Reiss, Katharina and Hans Vermeer (2014 [1984]) *Towards a General Theory of Translational Action: Skopos Theory Explained*, translated by Christiane Nord, Abingdon: Routledge.

Reynolds, Matthew (2016) *Translation: A Very Short Introduction*, Oxford: Oxford University Press.

Rose, Sue (2015) 'The Word Wizard', *The Linguist* 54(4): 18–19.

Samuel, Judith (2014) 'Shipshape in French', *The Linguist* 53(4): 24–25.

Sanders, Julie (2016) *Adaptation and Appropriation*, Abingdon: Routledge.

Schleiermacher, Friedrich (2012 [1813]) 'On the different methods of translating', in Lawrence Venuti (ed.) *The Translation Studies Reader* (Third Edition), Abingdon: Routledge, 43–63.

Shuttleworth, Mark and Moira Cowie (2014) *Dictionary of Translation Studies*, Abingdon: Routledge.

St. André, James (2006) '"He 'Catch No Ball' Leh!" Globalization versus Localization in the Singaporean Translation Market', *Meta* 51(4): 771–786.

Tanner, Nick (2013) 'Naked Chef Abroad', *The Linguist* 52(3): 12–13.

Tsujimura, Natsuko (2014) *An Introduction to Japanese Linguistics* (Third Edition), Chichester: Wiley Blackwell.

Tymoczko, Maria (2014) *Enlarging Translation, Empowering Translators*, Abingdon: Routledge.

Venuti, Lawrence (2008) *The Translator's Invisibility: A History of Translation* (Second Edition), Abingdon: Routledge.

Venuti, Lawrence (2012) *Translation Changes Everything: Theory and Practice*, Abingdon: Routledge.

Vermeer, Hans. J. (2012 [1989]) 'Skopos and Commission in Translational Action', translated by Andrew Chesterman, in Lawrence Venuti (ed.) *The Translation Studies Reader* (Third Edition), Abingdon: Routledge.

Vinay, Jean-Paul and Jean Darbelnet (1995 [1958]) *Comparative Stylistics of French and English: A Methodology for Translation*, translated and edited by Juan C. Sager and Marie-Jo Hamel, Amsterdam: John Benjamins.

Wakayabashi, Judy (2016) 'Script as a Factor in Translation', *Journal of World Literature* 1(2): 173–194.

Žižek, Slavoj (2016) *Antigone*, London: Bloomsbury.

Name Index

Subject Index